P9-BYE-399

The Best
Christian
Writing
❧ 2002

THE BEST
CHRISTIAN
WRITING
2002

SERIES EDITOR
JOHN WILSON

INTRODUCED BY
EUGENE PETERSON

A *Division of* HarperCollins*Publishers*

FIRST HARPERCOLLINS PAPERBACK EDITION PUBLISHED IN 2002

Library of Congress Cataloging-in-Publication Data has been ordered.

ISBN 0–06–009483–4

02 03 04 05 06 RRD(H) 10 9 8 7 6 5 4 3 2 1

CONTENTS

When I was gathering pieces for an earlier volume in this series, I wrote to a writer I've admired for many years, asking permission to include an essay of his. It was a terrific essay, one of the best I'd read in the past year, and I was eager to have it in the book. He responded very graciously, yet with bemusement. He hadn't thought of what he'd written as *Christian*, he said, and he couldn't imagine why anyone would want to assemble a collection of essays flying under that flag. A lively correspondence via e-mail ensued.

I've thought about that exchange now and then, most recently when reading Robert Benson's splendid book, *That We May Perfectly Love Thee: Preparing Our Hearts for the Eucharist.* Early in the book, Benson recalls some of the places where he has worshiped over the years, from the Nazarene churches in which he was raised to the Episcopal cathedral where he and his wife regularly worship today. These churches vary widely in the way they enact "the liturgical dance," in "architecture and symbolism and form." Each is different, distinctive, and yet they are all the same:

The truth, I have come to discover, is that I can wander into virtually any liturgical community—Catholic, Episcopalian, Lutheran, to mention some that I visit most frequently—on any given Sunday and be at home in a way that I never thought possible. Not at home in the sense of knowing everyone or being known by everyone there, but in the sense of being gathered together with all of those who call themselves Christians and who would worship the One Who made us.

Why a collection of "Christian writing"? To embody the unity in diversity that Benson evokes. These essays differ from one another not only insofar as they represent different traditions of Christian belief but also in the irreducible variousness of humanity: each person unique, one of a kind, yet each made expressly in the image of the triune God, Father, Son, and Holy Spirit.

Amy Schwartz, whose "Screwtape Instructs Scrapetooth" appears here as the winning entry in a contest co-sponsored by HarperCollins and belifefnet.com, writes as an observant Jew and a longtime reader of C. S. Lewis. Schwartz's mordant updating of Lewis' *Screwtape Letters* reminds us that some of the best Christian writing finds an audience outside the Christian community.

The other writers in this book are variously Christian: Protestant, Catholic, Orthodox. In our Father's house are many mansions.

As in past years, many people helped in the preparation of this volume. Thanks first to Steve Hanselman (who proposed the series), John Loudon, Gideon Weil, Roger Freet, Chris Hafner, and the rest of the staff of HarperSanFrancisco, who are proof that the classic virtues of publishing are alive and well. I would also like to thank David Heim, Miroslav Volf (who acted as a diplomatic courier), Elizabeth and Rick Wilson, Philip Yancey, and Phil Zaleski. Special thanks to Virginia Stem Owens and the rest of the Chrysostom Society for a weekend in the Texas hill-country, where I met Eugene and Jan Peterson for the first time. And finally: thank you, Wendy.

Eugene Peterson

Years ago I had a dog who had a fondness for large bones. Fortunately for him we lived in the forested foothills of Montana. In his forest rambles he often came across a carcass of a white-tailed deer that had been brought down by the coyotes. Later he would show up on our stone, lakeside patio carrying or dragging his trophy, usually a shank or a rib; he was a small dog and the bone was often nearly as large as he was. Anyone who has owned a dog knows the routine: he would prance and gambol playfully before us with his prize, wagging his tail, proud of his find, courting our approval. And, of course, we approved: We lavished praise, telling him what a good dog he was. But after a while, sated with our applause, he would drag the bone off twenty yards or so to a more private place, usually the shade of a large moss-covered boulder, and go to work on the bone. The social aspects of the bone were behind him; now the pleasure became solitary. He gnawed the bone, turned it over and around, licked it, worried it. Sometimes we could hear a low rumble or growl, what in a cat would be a purr. He was obviously enjoying himself and in no hurry. After a leisurely couple of hours he would bury it and return the next day to take it up again. An average bone lasted about a week.

I always took delight in my dog's delight, his playful seriousness, his childlike spontaneities now totally absorbed in "the one thing needful." But imagine my further delight in coming upon a phrase one day while reading Isaiah in which I found the poet-prophet observing something similar to what I enjoyed so much in my dog, except that his animal was a lion instead of a dog: ". . . as a lion or a young lion growls over his prey" (Isaiah 31.4). *Growls* is the word that caught my attention and brought me that little "pop" of delight. What my dog did over his precious bone, making those low throaty rumbles of pleasure as he gnawed, enjoyed, and savored his prize, Isaiah's lion did to his prey. The nugget of my delight was noticing the Hebrew word here translated "growl" (*hagah*) but usually translated "meditate," as in the Psalm 1 phrase describing the blessed man or woman whose "delight is in the law of the Lord on which he *meditates* day and night." Or in Psalm 63: "when I think of thee upon my bed, and *meditate* on thee in the watches of the night." But Isaiah uses this word to refer to a lion growling over his prey the way my dog worries a bone.

Hagah is a word that our Hebrew ancestors used frequently for reading the kind of writing that deals with our souls. But "meditate" is far too tame a word for what is being signified. Meditate seems more suited to what I do in a quiet chapel on my knees with a candle burning on the altar. Or my wife sitting in a rose garden with the Bible open in her lap. But when

Isaiah's lion and my dog meditated they chewed and swallowed, using teeth and tongue, stomach and intestines: Isaiah's lion meditating his goat (if that's what it was); my dog meditating his bone. There is a certain kind of writing that invites this kind of reading, soft purrs and low growls as we taste and savor, anticipate and take in the sweet and spicy, mouth-watering and soul-energizing morsel words—"O taste and see that the Lord is good!" Isaiah uses the same word (*hagah*) a few pages later for the cooing of a dove (38.14). One careful reader of this text caught the spirit of the word when he said that *hagah* means that a person "is lost in his religion," which is exactly what my dog was in his bone. Baron Friedrich von Hugel compared this way of reading to "letting a very slowly dissolving lozenge melt imperceptibly in your mouth."

I am interested in cultivating this kind of reading to match the kind of writing assembled in the chapters of this book. Writing designated "Christian" anticipates precisely this kind of reading—ruminative and leisurely, a dalliance with words in contrast to wolfing down information. Christian writers work under the shaping influence of Moses and Isaiah, Ezekiel and Jeremiah, Mark and Paul, Luke and John, Matthew and David, a "school" for writers marked by a trust in the "power of the words" (Coleridge's phrase) to keep us in touch with and responsive to reality, whether visible or invisible: God-reality, God-presence. Not all who attend the school graduate; there are many dropouts along the way. And more than a few come out with embarrassingly poor marks. But by keeping company

with the writers of Holy Scripture we are schooled in a practice of reading and writing that is infused with an enormous
respect—more than respect, awed reverence—for the revelatory and transformative power of words. The opening page of
the Christian text, the Bible, tells us that the entire cosmos
and every living creature are brought into being by words. St.
John selects the term *Word* to account, first and last, for what
is most characteristic about Jesus, the person at the revealed
and revealing center of the Christian story. Language, spoken
and written, is the primary means for getting us in on what is.
But it is language of a certain stripe, not words external to our
lives, the sort used in grocery lists, computer manuals, French
grammars, and basketball rule books, but words intended,
whether confrontationally or obliquely, to get inside us, to
deal with our souls. Such writing anticipates and counts on a
certain kind of reading, a dog-with-a-bone kind of reading.

Writers of other faith traditions and writers who hold to
none—atheists, agnostics, secularists—also, of course, have
access to this school (there are no admittance requirements) and
benefit enormously from its training in the holiness of words.
But the adjective *Christian* does serve to identify the way writers who collectively scribed the Bible used language to form
"the mind of Christ" in their readers. The adjective continues
to be useful in identifying the men and women who, as we
write our journalism and commentary, our studies and reflections, our stories and poems, continue to submit our imagina-
tions to the shaping syntax and diction of our biblical masters.

The identifying adjective *Christian* does not, obviously, confer any privilege or authority on the writer. And it doesn't so much as hint at rank or quality—there is plenty of mediocre and even bad writing by writers associated with our school. But the school itself, while not exactly unique, for its influence has spread far beyond its canonical walls, is persistently seminal in forming writers who honor words as holy, words as a basic means of forming an intricate web of relationship between God and the human, all things visible and invisible.

Neither does the adjective *Christian* when attached to the reader guarantee anything. But it does call attention to a way of reading that is congruent with Christian writing, reading appropriate to the writing that trusts in the power of words to penetrate our lives and create truth and beauty and goodness. This is the kind of reading named by our ancestors as *lectio divina*, often translated "spiritual reading"—reading that enters our souls as food enters our stomachs and becomes holiness and love and wisdom.

Christian writing needs Christian reading. Christian writing is stillborn without a reading that is Christian.

In 1916 a young Swiss pastor, Karl Barth, gave an address in the neighboring village of Leutwil where his friend Eduard Thurneyson was pastor. He was thirty years old, had been a pastor in Safenwil for five years, and was just beginning to discover the Bible. A few miles away the rest of Europe was on fire with war, a war epidemic with lies and carnage that marked what one writer at the time (Karl Kraus) called the "irreparable termination of what was humane in Western civilization." Each succeeding decade of the century supplied more details, political, cultural, and spiritual evidence of the world inexorably becoming what T. S. Eliot had laid out in prescient poetry as "The Waste Land."

At the time that the killing and lying were in full spate, just across the German and French borders in neutral Switzerland, this young pastor had discovered the Bible as if for the first time, discovered it as a book absolutely unique, unprecedented. The soul and body of Europe, and eventually the world, was being violated. On every continent millions were hanging on news from "the front" and on speeches from the world's leaders reported by the journalists. Meanwhile, Barth, in his small, out-of-the-way village, was writing what he had discovered—the extraordinary, truth-releasing, God-witnessing, culture-challenging realities in this book, the Bible. After a few years he published in his commentary, *Epistle to the Romans*, what he had discovered. It was the first in a procession of books that in the years to come would convince many Christians that the Bible was giving a truer, more accurate account of what was going on in their seemingly unraveling world than what their politicians and journalists were telling them. At the same time Barth determined to recover the capacity of Christians to *read* the book receptively in its original, transformative character. Barth brought the Bible out of the academic mothballs in which it had been stored for so long. He demonstrated how presently alive it is, and how different it is from books that can be "handled"—dissected and analyzed and then used for whatever we want them for. He showed, clearly and persuasively, that this "different" kind of writing (revelatory and intimate instead of informational and impersonal) must be met by a different kind of reading (receptive and leisurely instead of stand-offish and efficient). He also kept calling attention to writers who had absorbed and continued to write in the biblical style, involving us as readers in life-transforming responses. Dostoevsky and Genesis, for instance, as the Russian reproduced in his novels the radical Genesis reversals of human assessments, shaping his characters under the rubric of the divine "nevertheless" and not as the divine "therefore."

Later he published his Leutwil address under the title "The Strange New World Within the Bible." At a time and in a culture in which the Bible had been embalmed and buried by a couple of generations of undertaker-scholars, he passionately and relentlessly insisted that "the child is not dead but sleeping," took her by the hand, and said, "Arise." For the next fifty years, Barth demonstrated the incredible vigor and energy radiating from the sentences and stories of this Book and showed us how to read them.

Barth insists that we do not read this book and the subsequent writings that are shaped by it in order to find out how to get God into our lives, to get him to participate in our lives. No. We open this Book and find that page after page it takes us off guard, surprises us, and draws us into *its* reality, pulls us into participation with God on *his* terms.

He provided an illustration that became famous. I am using the germ of his anecdote but furnishing it, with a little help from Walker Percy, with my own details. Imagine a group of men and women in a huge warehouse. They were born in this warehouse, grew up in it, and have everything there for their needs and comfort. There are no exits to the building, only windows. But the windows have never been cleaned, and are thick with dust, and so no one bothers to look out. Why would they? The warehouse is everything they know and has everything they need. But then one day one of the children drags a stepstool under one of the windows, scrapes off the grime, and looks out. He sees people walking on the streets; he calls to his friends to come and look. They crowd around the window—they never knew a world existed outside their warehouse. And then they notice a person out in the street looking up and pointing; soon several people are gathered, looking up and talking excitedly. The children look up, but there is nothing to see but the roof of their warehouse. They finally get tired of watching these people out on the street acting crazily, pointing up at nothing and getting excited about it. What's the point of stopping for no reason at all, pointing at nothing at all, and talking up a storm about the nothing?

But what those people in the street were looking at was an airplane (or geese in flight, or a gigantic pile of cumulous clouds). The people in the street look up and see the heavens and everything in the heavens. The warehouse people have no heavens above them, just a roof.

What would happen, though, if one day one of those kids cut a door out of the warehouse, coaxed his friends out, and discovered the immense sky above them and the grand horizons beyond them? That is what happens, writes Barth, when we open the Bible—we enter the totally unfamiliar world of God, a world of creation and salvation stretching endlessly above and beyond us. Life in the warehouse never prepared us for anything like this.

Typically, adults in the warehouse scoff at the tales the children bring back. After all, they are completely in control in of the warehouse world in ways they could never be outside. And they want to keep it that way.

St. Paul was the little kid who first scraped the grime off the window for Barth, cut out a door, and coaxed him outdoors into the large "strange" world to which the biblical writers give witness. Under this school of writers, beginning with St. Paul, but soon including the entire faculty, Barth became a Christian *reader*, reading words in order to be formed by the Word. Only then did he become a Christian *writer*.

Barth's account of what had happened to him was later published in *The Word of God and the Word of Man*. John Updike said that that book "gave me a philosophy to live and labor by, and in that way changed my life." On receiving the Campion medal in 1997, Updike credited the Christian faith revealed in Barth's rediscovered Bible for telling him, as a writer, "that truth is holy, and truth-telling a noble and useful profession; that the reality around us is created and worth celebrating;

that men and women are radically imperfect and radically valuable."

The first metaphors for writing and reading that caught my fancy were from Kafka: "If the book we are reading does not wake us, as with a fist hammering on our skull, why then do we read it? . . . A book must be like an ice-axe to break the frozen sea within us." I wanted to write books like that, fisticuff books, ice-axe books. I wanted to wake people up and turn them inside out. I hardly noticed the violence in the metaphors; I wanted to *make a difference*. And then I was caught up short by Wendell Berry's question: "Did you finish killing / everybody who was against peace?" I realized that the violence implicit in the metaphors wasn't exactly suited to what I had in mind in wanting to use words to the glory of God. Maybe there is a better way to understand the employment of words in Christian writing.

And then I noticed that the most striking biblical metaphor for reading was St. John eating a book: "I . . . went to the angel and told him to give me the little scroll; and he said to me, 'Take it, and eat; it will be bitter to your stomach, but sweet as honey in your mouth.' So I took the little scroll from the hand of the angel and ate it; it was sweet as honey in my mouth, but when I had eaten it, my stomach was made bitter." Jeremiah and Ezekiel before him had also eaten books—a good diet it would seem for anyone who cares about reading words rightly.

For attention-getting, this is as good as Kafka any day, but as metaphor it is far better. St. John, this endlessly fascinating early church apostle and pastor and writer, walks up to the angel and says, "Give me the book." The angel hands it over, "Here it is; eat it, eat the book." And John does. He eats the book. He was pastor of seven little churches awash in the Roman world of sex and entertainment, power and violence. His task was to keep their faith intact, their discipleship ardent, their hope fresh against formidable odds. He wanted them to live, really live, outlive everyone around them. And so he did what writers do—he wrote a book. But first he read a book, not *just* read it—he ate it, got it into his nerve endings, his reflexes, his imagination. The book he ate was Holy Scripture. Assimilated in his worship and prayer, his imagining and writing, it then became the book he wrote, the first great poem in the Christian tradition and the concluding book of the Bible, The Revelation.

Reading is an immense gift, but only if the words are assimilated, taken into the soul—eaten, chewed, gnawed, received in unhurried delight. Words of men and women long dead, or separated by miles and/or years, come off the page and enter our lives freshly and precisely, conveying truth and beauty and goodness, words that God's Spirit has used and uses to breathe life into our souls. Our access to reality deepens into past centuries, spreads across continents. But this reading also carries with it subtle dangers. Passionate words of men and women spoken in ecstasy can end up flattened on the page and dissected with an impersonal eye. Wild words wrung out of excruciating suffering can be skinned and stuffed, mounted and labeled as museum specimens. The danger in all reading is that words will be reduced to information, to data. We silence the living voice and reduce words to what we can use for our pleasure and convenience and profit.

One psalmist mocked his contemporaries for reducing the living God who spoke and listened to them to a gold or silver thing-god that they could use:

> . . . those who make them are like them,
> so also are those who trust in them.

It's an apt warning for us still as we deal daily with the incredible explosion of information technology in which words are routinely debased into data. These words need rescuing.

Eat this book.

TEACHER
Eleven Notes
(From *The American Scholar*)

1

I have been a teacher for almost thirty years without having intended to be one. I suspect this is true of many of us. The postwar explosion of American schools—and their consolidation into a uniform, specialized institution, an industry—sucked up into the academy most of the other forms of high culture and their practitioners. People who hoped to be writers, painters, composers, performers, critics, and cultural journalists have ended up as teachers first and something else second. Or third: to be a teacher now means being a committeeperson, an academic politician, a conference goer, an administrator, a grant winner, a counselor. You'll be lucky if you paint a few weeks a year.

And you'll be lucky if it isn't academic painting, or painting enslaved by your rebellion against academic painting: "We are but critics, or but half create, / Timid, entangled, empty and abashed." Our residence in schools pays us something and costs us something. Everything in a school must be made scholastic. Thinking is pied into disciplines; teaching withers to the transfer of disciplinary methods. Painters talk about the theory of paint. Poets found journals to host theories of poetry; the theory comes back on the poetry and separates it from common speech. This is called the reflexivity of post-modern culture. In truth, it is the academy talking to itself. Art never confronts its only real criteria, the moral and narrative needs of practical life.

Which are dealt with, in the academy as in society as a whole, as matters of technique and money, whose criteria are feasibility and profit. In academicizing art and commercializ-ing the academy, we have had the support of society at large; we have had the urging, almost the demand, of the govern-ment. The humanities, Paul Goodman wrote, "cannot be taught in colleges at all," for there are no "veterans" of their practice—and this is because "free and learned thought is sim-ply not a social force among us," "the very notion of a nonaca-demic practice of history, philosophy, or humane letters [having] nearly vanished." Goodman wrote this in 1962; but he would have been equally right to say it of 1952 or 1942. Looking back, I have no idea, really, what the boundary date should be—only that we have been living under present con-ditions for so long that no practicing academic can remember anything different. Goodman himself represented the "public intellectuals" who appear on occasion and in special circumstances; but he was right to imply that such writers represent no established "practice" in society as a whole.

I had been a teacher for a long time when I went to a party at a distinguished private university and was called sharply to my senses. The talk was exclusively of package tours to cultural places, of programs accessed, of contracts angled for and jobs neatly wangled, of the food at the faculty club. It's possible that someone at some point mentioned a poem, to have others fumble for the title and not know it. The intellectual oxygen in the room wouldn't have sustained a match. I left early and came back to the farm. But I felt shaken and impatient for days.

2

Now, as the end of my career comes into view, I have started to weed out my files. They are full of weeds: repetitious copies of old syllabi and examinations, lecture notes, the material I have banked up against the passing of the semesters. I have told myself there would be something useful here, an idea or a phrase I might use in a serious way, when I had time. But I am embarrassed to read most of it, especially the syllabi. They strike me now as mannered, abrupt, and condescending. I suppose the mannerism was meant to be charming; the abruptness, concise and businesslike; the condescension, a challenge to student complacency. This is what I hope was true. I almost remember it that way.

I know teachers who have all their grade books lined up on a shelf, uniformly green, spiral-bound, each class, student, and grade inked into its box in the grid. The grade book is like an ore survey or a savings book, and there is a new book every year, twenty-five or thirty of them: the shelf is a monument.

I have never bothered with attendance. My theory has been that if my students found I was not helping them by what I said, they ought by rights to stay away. My grades have been recorded, in a numerical shorthand of my own device, on ordinary typing paper, on yellow legal sheets, and on the backs of memos.

I have never kept formal memorabilia and wonder now if this was a mistake. I think not. It would have been very hard for me, temperamentally, to collect such things, and therefore probably wrong to require it of myself. I wonder if, when I am eighty, I will wish I had letters of commendation, plaques, citations, photos, yearbooks, and commemorative pens. I won't have them, however, and that is that.

I do have a collection of random souvenirs that have accumulated more from a failure to purge them than from a decision to keep them. I have a matchbox of thorns given me when I taught the English romantics and remarked that "I fall upon the thorns of life! I bleed!" always struck me as comic. I have a small ceramic groundhog given me by a young man because I was his only teacher to know where Punxsutawney was (or how to spell it). I have an old bullet clip made during World War I for one of its standard rifles. I have a poster of heavy corrugated cardboard, hand-drawn for someone else in my first or second year of teaching. It reads, "An apple a day is pretty cheap pay." It is yellowed and stands warping on the baseboard heater.

I have a small wooden box with plastic windows and three papered rollers behind them—month, date, day. It has not recorded the correct day or date for twenty-five years, except when one of my daughters would fix it, with a sigh of exasperation, after which it would be correct for one day. No one registers dates in this job. It is important only that it is Tuesday or Wednesday, or even that it is Shakespeare day, and that you have glanced at *Antony and Cleopatra* again before you head down the hall.

3

I have begun to give away my books. Of course the shelves have always been in a slow flux. Publishers send samples, which I have routinely given away in preference to selling them to bootleg distributors. (Now the publishers print "Examination Copy" and "Not for Sale" in ribbons of color, like oriflammes, across the covers.) But I am beginning to give away books I once chose to acquire.

The odd thing is that, as I stand before the shelves, facing the jury, the covers that draw my eyes are the faded paperbacks I bought as an undergraduate. These are the ones I suspect I will be keeping. Not out of nostalgia: my schooling left none behind it. The impulse, I believe, is more that when you have only a little money and are just starting to read—when you know almost nothing, and know *that*—you buy Plato, Augustine, Nietzsche, Thoreau, the names you hear talked about. You don't buy *Existentializing the Asymptote: Bureaucracy and Hermaphroditism in the Late Works of. . . .* (You see how it is impossible even to parody these titles.) It doesn't occur to you that you might buy such things. They are books for libraries, and anyhow they are too expensive. You buy Lao Tzu, *Purgatorio*, *Heart of Darkness*, Yeats, Proust, Woolf.

I have claimed for years that the only books worth reading with a class are ones you can carry to class in your pocket. These are the ones becoming visible again. I feel some apprehension about this. These books may be a jury, but not a jury of my peers. They seem to call me to account, and I doubt that I can give an account. One thing university monographs can be used for is protection from writers like Plato, the ones as serious as Bach and Goya. But sooner or later you get tired of weaseling, I think. There seems to be health in sitting down again to read, "Near the end of March, 1845, I borrowed an axe. . . ."

Stanley Cavell is the only writer on Thoreau who realizes that *Walden* was a new scripture. The notion is oxymoronic. You can't really have a new scripture any more than you can have an ex-king or a former saint. What the oxymoron shows is the gravity of the demand placed on narrative, on sentences, finally on words, by Thoreau's notion of economy. To economize is to live a spartan life and to give an account of it. An account timely and exacting enough economizes on the pause between deed and word, until the word becomes the deed. The demand is almost intolerable: every word a real-time act of conscience. In *A Week on the Concord and Merrimack Rivers*, Thoreau could not live up to his own demand and was driven to go on, obsessively, unforgivably, hacking at his sentences in an effort to make an ideal, like friendship, clear enough to hazard himself on. By the time he wrote *Walden*, he had learned how to meet the demand with aphorism, which turns the demand aside and fulfills it by suggestion—that is, by transferring it to us. And Thoreau had learned to trust nature, which does not account for itself and need not. How much silence there is in *Walden!* Thoreau doesn't have to hurry. He won't miss the mail. *His axe is at the foot of the tree.*

But most of my books are nothing like *Walden*, of course, and I regret having bought them. They were expensive, profitless, and distracting. I bought many in fits of identification with the academy, which I hoped would become a home for me. But I have given up this aspiration. I have put my axe to a modest tree.

4

How students dress. Not long ago I told a class that their clothes constituted a uniform. It wasn't a substantive observation, just an illustration in passing, so I was surprised when a girl to my left broke out, interrupting me, angry, "No. I'd have to disagree with that."

Have to. I half-consciously registered the odd force of her words, but I answered just by looking demonstratively around the room, trusting that she and the others would see what I saw: every student except one was wearing light blue denim jeans and a sweatshirt and some brand of hiking boot. (It was perfectly pragmatic clothing: this was January in Michigan.) The only exceptions were one pair of black denims and one pair of economy low-top sneakers.

After looking around the circle, I said, "Well . . . ," hoping, expecting really, that the moment had answered the question, at least in terms of data—now we had all seen the same thing—and that I could ask where the demurral had come from and what it meant. But the girl was firm, glaring at me. (Directing my attention around the circle, I'm not sure whether she had followed my glance.) She had a cap of short red hair and eyes set too close, so that she seemed to be always frowning with anger or anxiety. She had metal beads tracking the edges of her ears and a metal stud in her tongue. For her, my demonstration had answered nothing.

So I said, "Well, everyone has jeans on. . . ."

"But that doesn't mean we're dressed the same way," she broke in again. "I mean, Ray isn't dressed like the rest of us."

"But he's the only one of you *not* wearing boots," I said.

"I still don't see why you think we're dressed the same," came the angry insistence again. I thought, "Because you are," but I had already fallen through the ice of lucid discourse and was floundering. I could have dismissed the day's topic and focused on her anger. But I don't go in for classroom humiliations or public therapy, and no one else, not even Ray, seemed to be interested.

Why was she angry? What were we talking about? Was it that I had bent the students' attention back on themselves? Was it that my look, which I had meant to be frank and open, seemed arrogant and objectifying? Was she angry because she had to be there at all? Then she wasn't angry at *me*. I suspect we were perturbed by the same fact, how the market in clothes (as in food and ideas) furnishes us all virtually identically; and how intense a denial of human particularity this entails.

The truth is I wear a uniform myself—khakis, flannel shirt—and so whatever experimentation occurs is carried out by students. One day (another class, another semester) the sweatshirt arrived with a long pleated skirt and granny boots, and a thick cable-knit cap of unbleached wool. The student being male, the effect was monastic, Tibetan. Just eccentricity, as it turned out.

This is Michigan, as I have said, but they wear their heavy down jackets open in front, with the sleeves slid down over their hands. It is as if they were insisting on powerlessness, miming having no hands or arms, only wings.

Here are a short skirt, black stockings, and high heels teetering through the slush in the parking lot. This is perhaps just a miscalculation on its way to an audition. One day I watched a black cocktail dress, long earrings touching and touching the elegant neck, and a two-handed tub of Mountain Dew.

You can't disguise the necks or make them any less child-like—and there, also, the ponytails and pigtails and the tiny braids as delicate as caterpillars.

5

The basic equipment for a classroom teacher is the same as for a stand-up comedian: a striking voice, a direct gaze, and the inner freedom to say more or less anything that comes to mind. Also useful is a thick mental deposit of miscellaneous information: anecdotes, publication dates and other historical clutter, phrases from songs, the names and saleable features of recent movie figures all stick involuntarily in my mind and are subject to random, improvisatory recall.

What you do with this equipment depends, of course, on whether you can remain intellectually and emotionally open, vital. Since the time I took the required degrees and was, in this way, licensed to practice, I have read a great deal, partly because I love the English language and the things made of it, and partly because the habit of formal discourse was implanted in me very young. Criticism has flavors as poetry does. But I doubt if a large body of systematic knowledge is of much use to a teacher of undergraduates. Which means that much of our formal professional training is beside the point. Changes of critical or pedagogical method provide topics for conferences, but I doubt if students are cumulatively much better (or worse) readers and writers than they ever were.

That isn't what's going on in the classroom.

What's going on is partly waiting. You talk with and to students, waiting for the moment of intellectual shock, or fear, or (more rarely) love, that means something has found its way in, or been allowed in, though the significance of this is the student's to state and may not be evident for years. This is, mind you, *intellectual* fear or love—but the exact relation or interchange between thought and feeling is impossible to state. There is a decorum here. The classroom is not a therapy session, and I have no use for those who turn it into one—or into a professedly egalitarian market of personal (usually sexual) relations—and then prey on people.

Yet *there are people present:* a complicated hermeneutic, private and public, is being carried on, in which the text you are discussing is only a knot, or an occasion. And the results of the hermeneutic practice are always in code.

I lecture and overhear myself. Some of what I say is foreknown, preowned, cadged at random. Some is exploratory: I'm looking for, looking out for, a sharper phrase for the notion at hand. Some of what I say has no intellectual purpose but is simply to punctuate the time, to let us relax. I tell a story, or note something I saw on the way to class and reflect on it for a moment, or pause at a pun that has cropped up, or clown about the administration's hidden microphone and greet the dean, loudly, into the radiator.

And this lecturing, this line, this snake oil, has to do with my own psychological continuity and security as well as with *Lear* or the construction of paragraphs. I am one of the people present—and in sharper need than the students because I am older and have fewer options. (Odd that the pretense should be that I can offer *them* options.) The forward momentum of my speech is running one story above the more complicated back-and-forth movement of my colloquy with myself (and the same is true of their listening), I am coping with the powerful reality of these young humans in the room with me, I am trying to cope with the increasing embarrassment of encountering my own limitations. It is an odd, quite specific mode of living.

And what will I do when these brief, regular performances are no longer requested? No one has told me this, but I suspect that the most frightening thing about retirement may be the sudden stillness of one's own voice. A few of us, very few, will be invited to schools and conferences to go on talking and put off the day of silence. Most of us will just have to go home and be silent. How will we get along with ourselves?

6

I walk through the small library at all hours. Students sit at tables, isolated by reading. A girl is sleeping in a carrel, cheek on forearms, her dark hair rumpled and sweaty.

I feel tenderness toward them. This is because I have grown older on the job. When I began teaching they were more or less my equals—rivals, friends, enemies, sexual possibilities. But they have remained the same age, while I have run in a panic through my life. They have been stable; I have been unstable. They have remained faithful; I am the traitor.

Teaching is an encounter with death, more palpably and immediately than philosophy is. (But then for Plato teaching and philosophy were not clearly separable.) Walking through the classroom door reminds you that you are about to expend fifty more minutes out of your limited supply. You can feel them leaving as you speak. Teaching is a real-time affair: its substance is the changes that may occur, in any of you, as you live through the minutes you use. As you live, of course, you change. But some of the changes are deliberate, occasioned, and these change the living you do next.

Other forms of labor highlight the passing of time as well, but teaching more so, because its medium is typically language. Words don't stay in the world for long. They fade instantly, like piano tones. And we can have (in the nature of the thing) only a deflected and fragmented knowledge of their effects on others. So there is a recurrent moment, as I walk away from class—for me, at least, more usually after a good class—when someone calls after me down the hall and I flinch, deeply, viscerally, and then shrug off the salutation with a violent internal shudder. The call is not too much to be borne but too much to be borne patiently or peaceably. *Nos morituri.* Don't remind me.

7

Maybe students are aware of this, I don't know (or recall), and this is why they fasten on us the stereotype of "The Old Prof." Mr. Chips. The teacher in *Dead Poets Society.* It may be the same sentimentality we use to keep from acknowledging that our parents will die. But such images also recapitulate the determination of our society not to be moved by thought. The image assimilates the teacher, making her just a function of the neutered academic myth, though she may in fact have lived her whole intellectual life in rebellion against both the academic myth and its sponsoring culture. *Dead Poets Society*—this explains its popularity—has it both ways: the martyred teacher rebels against a tyrannical administration in favor of a commonplace educational liberalism that any actual dean would be delighted with.

As for Chips, he is appalling. He is a blunderer without interest in his subject, the perfectly obsequious instrument of his cultural place and time. In the sixth section of Hilton's story, Chips is visited by a former ghetto boy, now a soldier (it is early in World War I). The soldier wants to thank Chips for organizing an outing to the public school years earlier. "One o' the best days aht I ever 'ad in me life," he says in his cute and deplorable accent, and then is erased to a grateful blur in Chips's memory by a sweet and comely death at Passchendaele.

There is a Ms. Chips as well, sexless but maternal (or sororal), devoted to literature or simply, like Chips, to the existence *in perpetuam* of her school. And an Anti-Chips: students will idealize a mentor in cynicism, though it is not unheard-of that, as the career draws to a close, Anti-Chips will reveal the essential sentimentality of his identity by attracting, or even desiring, the guise of Chips himself.

They are all avoidances of death—that is, of the facts of the classroom—whether assigned by students or desired and connived by teachers. They are also guild markings, professional manners. Sometimes, I suspect, they are camouflage for a genuine vocation. Sift the genuine teachers out of the institutional mix of grant winners, politicians, and computer mavens, and you will find them using different apparent adjustments to the system. The desire to teach because it is one's calling needs disguise now, because it is so thoroughly exploitable.

8

And it has become desperately complex, largely because of our ambivalence about authority. Teaching is, among other things, a use of, an appeal to, authority—inasmuch as a correct date or a clear distinction has authority, limits what we are free to think. We are not wrong to be suspicious of claims to authority: that sleepwalking charmer, Chips, was part of the ideological production of the victims of Passchendaele. But unless there is no clear distinction between a clear distinction and a blow to the mouth, we must have the authority of the one to set, as our only real academic retort, against the other.

Has anyone stated the complexity that our confusion about authority introduces into the classroom? I am speaking, still, of the experience of genuine teachers. They inform and distinguish and enforce. They also perform and enact, even entertain. But this work has become impossibly self-conscious. For the pretense is that the students are educating themselves. The teacher is paid to provide knowledge, planning, intellectual technique, encouragement, discipline, and evaluation, all potent enough to produce miracles and self-effacing enough to convince the students that they are doing everything themselves. Of course there are geniuses of this pretense; but on them the demands seem impossibly high. I think this explains the exhaustion that so frequently overtakes teachers after a decade's work, and the number of them who finish out in mechanical indifference what began as a morally exemplary calling.

We use up teachers by demanding the impossible from them, and we do this because we demand something impossible from education as a whole—to redeem society from the consequences of our quite deliberate plans for it. Since World War II, American culture has been redesigned for the comfort of the corporation. We have undercut the influence of other social institutions, families, churches, unions, and professions, in order to discourage the formation of any intellectual or moral independence that might question what corporations do. Not even corporations, however, can function in the resulting anomie. They too need reserves of informed, intellectually self-reliant, liberal, nonracist, nongenderist people. We have demanded, therefore, that the schools provide these people *ex nihilo*, or at least without the fabric of an intellectual and moral culture. Schools, after all, unlike families and churches, are supported by taxes. Let them do their work.

But schools cannot redeem society; the redemption, whatever it might entail, must go the other way. Of the postwar criticisms of American education that retain interest, Goodman's may be the best, because he understood the priority of culture as a whole. "Fundamentally," he wrote, "there is no right education except growing up into a worthwhile world." The pressure we put on schools, to create, by themselves, a "worthwhile world" is mainly a way of avoiding the practical corollary of Goodman's principle—that we must reform the other institutions of our culture before schools can resume their proper function.

But it is evident to the dimmest undergraduate that money and technological advance rule the social world, and that schools have influence only insofar as they fall in line. The pretense that students teach themselves is only a disguise for the education they have received before coming to school, and the themes of this earlier, deeper education are money and technological advance. That everyone must "receive the benefits of higher education" in identical schools merely levels the field for the corporations. It guarantees that these candidates for employment will have had the proper training. No political ferment or wayward moral acuteness will ruck up the turf.

9

In his autobiographical reflections, *A Pitch of Philosophy*, Cavell speaks of "the trauma of the birth of culture in oneself," and it seems to me that I recognize this event, or sign, in myself, and that the wound of it has never healed. For me, as for Cavell, it came in part from music. For me—as not, I take it, for Cavell—it came also from poetry and in church.

This experience and its sources seem worth exploration, because they may help to explain why I went on teaching. That the birth of faith—the second birth—may be traumatic will be obvious even to those who have not read Kierkegaard, though he is the classic expositor and dramatist of the fact for us. But faith has an ambivalent relation to culture—both antithetical to it and creative of it, as river source to river mouth or the throw of dice to the score. Belief teaches you that life carries demands that cannot be finessed or negotiated. Then you discover that serious music (for instance) makes this same kind of demand, which is why it often has a religious source or reach. Bach's work will make no allowances for you; you can't make easy friends with it; it takes away your self-assurance. Now your assurance must come from having lived up to its demands—but you cannot, and so the wound never heals.

That belief and music make similar demands does not, of course, mean that they always act in concord. Belief may require that one give up chorales and epics and other modes of normal cultural life. The life of faith means, in part, standing ready to do so. This is what Nietzsche called "the ascetic ideal" and why he saw art as opposed to it. It was not so much that he thought we should choose art over religion, as that he saw art as transcending the necessity of choosing. The moment you must choose between things of great value and things of ultimate value was, for Kierkegaard, the birth of ethical consciousness, and Nietzsche was determined to deny that moment its power. For him it was to be replaced by "lying," heroic fabrication, the source both of art and of the basic forms of culture.

Nietzsche's idea has been recently popular, at least in the humanities, because it lets us see academic work as having a form of ultimate value without tying us to belief. Not having undergone the birth of culture in school—neither church nor my encounters with serious music and poetry owed anything to school—I have never been more than a sojourner in the academy. This is in great part why I have chosen to remain a teacher of undergraduates. The higher you go in the attics of the American university, at least, the more professionalized the project becomes, and the less likely it is that you will encounter someone, as George Steiner says, "proudly sick with thought, hooked," or sick with the desire of thinking—or wounded with music, or willing to be wounded.

But where is Cavell in this, and what has his trauma cost? Further on in *A Pitch of Philosophy*, he speaks of the fact that "philosophy cannot have the grounding that it seeks" and suggests that "perhaps it will find a cure or a close." Philosophy here stands in for the aspirations of art and faith as well. The birth of culture traumatizes because we see there is no alternative to culture—that following out our lines of inquiry will never bring us to heaven or even to earth ("grounding"). We may hope for a "cure or a close," however, as we value the "intellectual companionship" on the way. But what would the intellectual companions do if culture did find its cure? What would we do with Harvard?

It is interesting to me, in this regard, that Cavell should turn so often to Thoreau and Emerson. Neither was a university mind, and Cavell strikes me as having an ideal (if exceptionally subtle and brilliant) university mind. Though the rigor of his attention to language sometimes sounds revolutionary, this is (I think) a dividend he is drawing from his texts, especially from Thoreau. The paragraph that begins with trauma ends with a reflection considerably less climactic and demanding—that Cavell's work serves a "perspective from which . . . [the] options and objects with which the world is conversant make the world in which, and in terms of which, to choose." This is sly: "world" here is so equivocal as to be a pun. Worldliness constitutes the "world" of thought, yet it excludes *the world*, that entity of illimitable time and elaboration in which you never know what is around the corner. But Cavell draws on "world" in this larger sense as well. For what his choosing means to achieve is "a small alteration" by which "the world"— this is THE world?—"might be taken a small step—or half step—toward perfection." This is what I would call negotiating with the nonnegotiable. Such half steps are not at all what Thoreau meant when he demanded his harrowing moral economy. I do not credit this kind of perfection. I do not think, I have never believed, the wound of culture (or of faith) could be ameliorated.

10

These notes may sound like evidence of disillusionment or discouragement. I do in fact feel these things, but not toward the possibility of teaching itself, only toward the academic world in which I have chanced to spend my professional life, the postwar academy drafted by Milton Eisenhower and Clark Kerr into the service of our lethal economy. Teaching constituted, or circumstanced, in a different way might be a noble thing.

Yet it is, under present conditions, the object of utopian vision only. Goodman knew this, I believe, yet insisted that "we should be experimenting with different kinds of school, no school at all, the real city as school, farm schools, practical apprenticeships, guided travel, work camps, little theaters and local newspapers, community service." Such a suggestion envisions a working intellectual culture diffused through society, with local peculiarities and traditions of learning—the very kind of culture the global university has always known it must destroy.

"If a man has had one teacher in his life," my father said to me one day, out of the blue, "he can consider himself lucky." He had two, and has never ceased to speak of them with respect and intensity, as if, now that he is in his eighties, they are still looking over his shoulder. But then he is a violinist and a composer, and his education owed almost nothing to the standard American schooling of his day. His teachers were, in a sense, his parents; they brought forth in him an exacting, precise set of skills, a wisdom, a responsibility, a knowledge of artistic right and wrong, that they had inherited from their teachers as a form of love.

Someone—I think the cellist Bernard Greenhouse—has left a picture of Pablo Casals teaching. Knees to knees with the young cellist, Casals plays a phrase from the Bach unaccompanied suites, and then pauses while the student plays it. "No," Casals says, and plays it again. The student plays it again. "No," Casals says, this time perhaps with a comment or a joke, and plays it again. And so on for the whole lesson.

This is more like it. The teaching is urgent, intense, and full of character. Yet the personalities involved are in a sense beside the point. The people, their entire selves, skill, talent, feeling, memory, moral and political commitments, are inextricable from the performance of the phrase, and yet are not the end of the exercise but merely the means. They are gates in the river of the ongoing performance of Bach's vision, or audition.

I never had a teacher at all, by this criterion or anything like it—there were intelligent and well-meaning people, of course, but not this. Nor have I had students—or exceedingly few—who would have put up with such teaching. I don't blame my students: Casals's teaching would be unjust in my classroom, because it would violate the expectations on which the classroom has been premised and the fee paid. My students have expected the teaching their cultural world requires, the bland, undemanding, rather mechanical, rather good-humored obedience to the state-supervised curriculum—and, of course, the pretense that the students are finding their own way to its conclusions. Neither Casals's rigor nor his anarchism would be appropriate here. Occasionally I have felt my classroom talk growing taut with something like his intensity. My students have generally responded with bewilderment. Perhaps this should not have stopped me. Perhaps there have been moments when my effort to be morally and verbally accountable in public, in speech, has had an effect. I have no record of such moments. I don't know how they would be recorded: academic record keeping is not tuned to them. So it is up to others to say.

11

Having admitted that my vision of teaching is utopian, I will indulge it further.

I would be glad to teach in a college that printed its catalogue on one side of a sheet of typing paper, one course of study for everyone, for one fee. I would be glad if there were room on the sheet, after the formalities, for Nietzsche's sentence about scholarship, from *The Birth of Tragedy* ("For the first time in history someone had *come to grips* with scholarship—and what a formidable, perplexing thing it turned out to be!"), and perhaps a few measures from *The Art of Fugue.*

The curriculum of this school would be chosen and rationalized by the faculty acting under the rule of consensus. All texts would, of course, be carried to class in the pocket. The canon of these texts would be variable. Those who dream of a one-culture canon have not considered what an enormous multicultural grab Homer and Bach represent in themselves.

I would be glad to teach in a school whose new president was inaugurated in ten minutes between classes, standing up with the trustees and anyone else who was free, all in everyday clothes. The new president could promise to do her best. As sometimes happens, I understand, in Quaker schools, she could leave her office door open to visitors as she worked.

In my ideal school, scholarly writing (or essays like this) would be limited to one piece every few years. Or we could establish a ration book system in which one teacher could trade coupons with another who had a book to write, in return for the right to five or ten years' silent thinking. This way many fewer books would be written. Most would be short enough to be accommodated in small paperbound form. Otherwise the college would keep a copy for the stacks.

In my school, the faculty would include a practicing homemaker, midwife, carpenter, businessperson, plumber, farmer, forester, and string quartet. I could have my office, as a teacher of poetry, in the physics or economics department. Or we could pick offices at random, by lot, every semester. We wouldn't have many books to move from office to office, and the ones we had would be light.

J. BOTTUM

THE GHOST OF CHRISTMAS PAST
Charles Dickens's Triumph

(From *The Weekly Standard*)

It's almost impossible not to know how it opens. "Marley was dead: to begin with. There is no doubt whatever about that." Charles Dickens's *A Christmas Carol* has been filmed at least forty-two times and dramatized for the stage in dozens of versions—the first almost immediately after the book's publication in 1843, a pirated play that Dickens spent £700 in court costs fighting before he won an uncollectable judgment against its producers (and thereby found material for the great Chancery case of *Jarndyce* v. *Jarndyce* that lies at the center of *Bleak House*, but that's another story). "Old Marley was as dead as a door-nail," the famous first paragraph of *A Christmas Carol* ends.

But who remembers how the second paragraph runs? "Mind! I don't mean to say that I know, of my own knowledge, what there is particularly dead about a door-nail. I might have been inclined, myself, to regard a coffin-nail as the deadest piece of ironmongery in the trade. But the wisdom of our ancestors is in the simile; and my unhallowed hands shall not disturb it, or the Country's done for. You will therefore permit me to repeat, emphatically, that Marley was as dead as a door-nail."

You don't get much of that narrator's voice in the films we've all seen, over and over, every Christmas—with Alastair Sim in the 1951 version, or George C. Scott in the 1984 version, or Mr. Magoo in the 1962 cartoon, for that matter. You don't get the wordiness: "I don't mean to say that I know, of my own knowledge, what there is particularly." You don't get the facetiousness: "my unhallowed hands shall not disturb it, or the Country's done for." You don't get the hallucinogenic animation of inanimate objects. You don't get the comedy running over and under the sentimentality. You don't get the manic speed, or the almost insane energy, or the sheer delight in writing down words. You may get the story—but you don't get Dickens.

And as for that story, it is, on its face, a considerable mess. Of course, we don't demand much coherence from the tale, which is in itself a revealing fact about the success of Dickens's art. His friend, unofficial agent, and biographer, John Forster, claimed that Dickens took a "secret delight" in giving "a higher form" to nursery stories, and the fairy-tale quality is one of the things the reader feels immediately in *A Christmas Carol*. You'd no more complain of its creaky plot than you'd demand greater structural integrity for *Rumpelstiltskin*.

But the story isn't what anyone would call tight. After talking to Marley's ghost until "past two" in the morning, Scrooge "went straight to bed, without undressing," only to awake to meet the Ghost of Christmas Past at midnight—two hours before he fell asleep and "clad but slightly in his slippers, dressing-gown, and nightcap."

Well, as the reformed Scrooge says on Christmas morning, "The Spirits have done it all in one night. They can do anything they like. Of course they can." One feels pedantic objecting to the illogic of ghosts, but in *A Christmas Carol* they behave more inconsistently than even ghosts deserve. Apparently nothing the poor Ghost of Christmas Yet To Come shows Scrooge comes true. Bob Cratchit won't weep, "My little, little child! . . . My little child!" at the memory of his departed son—for at the story's end, after Scrooge's reformation, we are assured that Tiny Tim "did not die." The new Scrooge will presumably meet his own death not alone, his very shirt and bed curtains stolen from around his corpse, but surrounded by his adoring nephew Fred, Fred's wife, Fred's wife's plump sister, and Tiny Tim, to whom he became "a second father."

Even the Ghost of Christmas Present doesn't manage to get much right. The guests at Fred's Christmas party won't make fun of Scrooge, because Scrooge will be there. The Cratchits won't have their little goose, "eked out by applesauce and mashed potatoes." They'll have instead the enormous "prize turkey" Scrooge has sent: "He never could have stood upon his legs, that bird. He would have snapped 'em short off in a minute, like sticks of sealing-wax." John Sutherland, the marvelous solver of minor literary problems in such books as *Was Heathcliff a Murderer?* and *Who Betrays Elizabeth Bennett?*, has a funny little note about the problems the family faced roasting that turkey. No wonder Bob Cratchit was a "full eighteen minutes and a half, behind his time" at work the next morning. The monstrous thing couldn't have been fully cooked until almost midnight. And didn't the Cratchits wonder where their meal had come from? For that matter, what is the poultry shop doing "half open" at six on Christmas morning—and why hasn't the poulterer already sold his prize bird, which, intended for a Christmas feast, is going to go bad in very short order?

Meanwhile, the characters are as unconvincing as the plot. The critic Edmund Wilson once suggested that the solution to the main figure's psychology lies in recognizing that Scrooge is a deeply divided man who will shortly revert to his miserliness. But even to speak of "Scrooge's psychology" is to miss the point, like demanding to see character development in Little Red Riding Hood and the big, bad wolf.

And yet, neither is Scrooge simply a placeholder for a fairy tale's moral of conversion. He was probably intended to be that, but Dickens can't leave him alone. Scrooge has far too much energy, takes far too much joy in being joyless. "If I could work my will . . . every idiot who goes about with 'Merry Christmas' on his lips, should be boiled with his own pudding, and buried with a stake of holly through his heart." "You may be an undigested bit of beef, a blot of mustard, a crumb of cheese, a fragment of an underdone potato," he says to Marley's ghost. "There's more of gravy than of grave about you, whatever you are!" He's Ralph Nickleby and Arthur Gride, the businessmen villains of *Nicholas Nickleby*, ratcheted up too much to be a mere marker of villainy—just as after his conversion, he's *Nicholas Nickleby*'s Cheeryble brothers, or Fezziwig from his own past, cranked up in absolutely insane glee: "Shaving was not an easy task, for his hand continued to shake very much; and shaving requires attention, even when you don't dance while you are at it."

But it isn't just Scrooge that Dickens can't leave alone. He can't leave anything alone, which is exactly what ends up making *A Christmas Carol* a triumph: the energy, the madness, the darting from thing to thing, the extravagance invested in every moment. George Orwell spotted this in Dickens. There are thousands of named characters in his fiction, and every single one of them has more put in him than necessary.

Even the unnamed characters can't help becoming Dickensian. While Scrooge and the Ghost of Christmas Past watch old Fezziwig's party, "In came the cook, with her brother's particular friend, the milkman. In came the boy from over the way, who was suspected of not having board enough from his master, trying to hide himself behind the girl from next door but one." Why do we have to know all this? Dickens is like some mad magician, incapable of *not* transforming each thing that happens to catch his eye. In the obituary he wrote for the *Times* when Dickens died, Anthony Trollope seemed almost to complain about how unfair it was: every other novelist has to bend his fiction to match reality, while reality bent itself to match Dickens; by the time he was done creating a fictional bootboy like Sam Weller or a fictional miser like Scrooge, real bootboys and misers turned themselves into Dickens's characters.

The various theories that dominated twentieth-century criticism never quite figured out what to do with Dickens. The literary Edwardians detested him for what they thought of as his sentimentality, his indulgence of the grotesque, and his female characters desexualized into "legless angels"—and also for his Victorian energy, so alien to their own ironic lethargy. There were moments during the century when Freudian interpretation seemed to grant some real insights into literature (although, as Harold Bloom put it, one always felt that Shakespeare was a better reader of Freud than Freud was of Shakespeare). But one of the reasons Freudianism failed as a theory of literary interpretation is that it could never get its arms around Dickens: he didn't seem to have any psychology at all in his books—just psychological truth.

Social criticism, in its turn, tried to claim Dickens as merely the unsystematic version of Marx and Engels, and *A Christmas Carol* as simply the more popular version of *The Condition of the Working Classes in England in 1844*. Even more sensible critics did little better and consistently preferred to think about authors like William Makepeace Thackeray and George

Eliot. Louis Cazamian found hardly anything in Dickens besides a *philosophie de Noël*. Orwell knew in his bones that Dickens was an author "worth fighting for," and yet he finally had to argue against Scrooge's conversion, on the grounds that Dickens never grasped the social, instead of the personal, structure of evil. F. R. Leavis painted himself into such a corner that he ended up insisting *Hard Times* was Dickens's most important work. Even critics as good as Edmund Wilson and Lionel Trilling didn't really succeed: they were too honest to deny that Dickens was, like Shakespeare, the great writer of his age, and then they went back to reading authors on whom they could actually use their gifts.

Curiously, postmodernism managed better, not in its multi-cultural aspect of race, class, and gender, but in its fascination with language—for one of the things that makes Dickens run is language. Think of the names in his fiction: Scrooge and Jarndyce and Betsy Trotwood and Oliver Twist. And think of his propensity for describing inanimate objects with the adjectives of life. It is the "higher form" of nursery stories, for Dickens needn't bother with brooms and wardrobes magically come alive. The life and the magic are in the words. In the Cratchits' kitchen, the "potatoes, bubbling up, knocked loudly at the saucepan-lid to be let out and peeled." Scrooge has "a gloomy suite of rooms, in a lowering pile of building up a yard, where it had so little business to be, that one could scarcely help fancying it must have run there when it was a young house, playing at hide-and-seek with other houses, and have forgotten the way out again."

The most Dickensian moment early in *A Christmas Carol* comes when Scrooge arrives home in the evening to see Marley's face in his door-knocker: "He did pause, with a moment's irresolution, before he shut the door; and he did look cautiously behind it first, as if he half expected to be terrified with the sight of Marley's pigtail sticking out into the hall." English literature has had perhaps a dozen authors who could or would have done the door-knocker. Only Dickens is capable of the pigtail.

When the Ghost of Christmas Present arrives, Dickens squanders five hundred words (out of twenty-eight thousand) describing a fruiter's and a grocer's shops:

> There were great, round, pot-bellied baskets of chestnuts, shaped like the waistcoats of jolly old gentlemen, lolling at the doors, and tumbling out into the street in their apoplectic opulence. There were ruddy, brown-faced, broad-girthed Spanish Onions, shining in the fatness of their growth like Spanish Friars, and winking from their shelves in wanton slyness at the girls as they went by, and glanced demurely at the hung-up mistletoe. There were . . . Norfolk Biffins, squab and swarthy, setting off the yellow of the oranges and lemons, and, in the great compactness of their juicy persons, urgently entreating and

beseeching to be carried home in paper bags and eaten after dinner.

That phrase "the great compactness of their juicy persons" could be imitated if one tried. Most parodies of Dickens get no further than the Dickensian sentimentality and *philosophie de Noël.* But it was this sort of odd, wordy construction that James Joyce, with his infallible eye, seized upon when he reached Dickens in the historical parodies of English prose that make up the maternity chapter of *Ulysses.* And the truth is that Dickens's language could be peculiar; this is the man who gave English the phrase "our mutual friend," when what he meant was a shared or common friend.

What can't be imitated is the energy. The Edwardians were right about Dickens's Victorianism—except that he was a hyper-Victorian, with all the virtues and vices of his age raised to something like the platonic ideal by the enormous power of his stamina. The biographer Edgar Johnson seems wrong when he says that Christmas has for Dickens only "the very smallest connection with Christian theology or dogma." There's plenty of Christianity in the Christmas books, from the preface, in which Dickens claims his purpose was to write "a whimsical kind of masque" that might "awaken some loving and forbearing thoughts, never out of season in a Christian land," to the most sentimental moment in *A Christmas Carol,* in which Tiny Tim "hoped the people saw him in the church, because he was a cripple, and it might be pleasant to them to remember upon Christmas Day, who made lame beggars walk, and blind men see."

But Johnson is at least right that the secularizing impulse has begun its implacable work. Even G. K. Chesterton, normally Dickens's most consistent promoter, complained that Dickens, faced with the single event around which the world has developed the most mythology, decided to invent his own Christmas mythology. But that's because traditional Christmas images actually involve the Christ who will become the Savior with his death and resurrection, and Dickens always wanted to avoid the hard cosmological edges of Christian theology. To read *The Life of Our Lord* that Dickens wrote for his own children is to think the key moment in Christian history is Christmas, not Easter, and the key teaching of Jesus is "Suffer little children, and forbid them not to come unto me: for of such is the kingdom of heaven." This is a massive diminishment of what St. Paul knew was the scandal of Christianity, but it's very Victorian—a reflection of all that was advanced, generous, liberal, high-minded, and doomed in the Gladstonian vision of a modern Christian state. "English flatheads" and "little moralistic females à la George Eliot," Nietzsche called them, who thought they could preserve Christian morality without much Christian religion.

In the months before *A Christmas Carol* was written in 1843, the serial publication of *Martin Chuzzlewit* had not been going well, the first of Dickens's full novels to receive less than universal acclaim. His sending of his characters young Martin and

Mark Tapley off to America helped, and the book gradually "forced itself up in people's opinion." But Dickens lived on his popularity; he needed esteem, and the tepid response to *Martin Chuzzlewit* brought home to him just how tired he was. He was supporting a huge household beyond his income, he had to act as his own promoter and copyright protector, and he had written six major novels in seven years. "It is impossible to go on working the brain to that extent for ever," he told Forster. "The very spirit of the thing, in doing it, leaves a horrible despondency behind."

So he decided, in cold, commercial calculation, that he would write a Christmas story and make the £1,000 he needed to take his family away to Italy for a long vacation. Of course, being Dickens, he couldn't leave it alone. He began *A Christmas Carol* early in October and completed it before the end of November—while, as he described it in a letter, he "wept and laughed, and wept again, and excited himself in a most extraordinary manner in the composition; and thinking whereof he walked about the black streets of London fifteen and twenty miles many a night when all sober folk had gone to bed." Demanding to oversee every aspect of publication, he forced upon his publisher expensive plates and bindings, and although the book's first printing of six thousand copies sold out in a single day, the initial quarter's profits brought him less than a third of the money he was hoping for.

That, too, was Dickens. As prolific an author as there has ever been, he was always living not on what he had done, but on money received for the promise of his next book. When *A Christmas Carol* was finished, he "broke out like a madman," with "such dinings, such dancings, such conjurings, such blind-man's-bluffings, such theatre-goings, such kissings-out of old years and kissings-in of new ones [as] never took place in these parts before. . . . And if you could have seen me at the children's party at Macready's the other night . . ."

Jane Carlyle did see him at that party for the actor William Charles Macready's children. She hadn't slept well for weeks—hadn't slept at all for two nights—and she was quarreling again with her husband, Thomas Carlyle. But once there, she found herself, like everyone else, caught up in the Dickensian world. "Dickens and Forster, above all, exerted themselves till the perspiration was pouring down and they seemed *drunk* with their efforts," she described it in a letter.

> Only think of that excellent Dickens playing the *conjuror* for one whole hour—the *best* conjuror I ever saw. . . . Then the dancing . . . the gigantic Thackeray &c &c all capering like *Maenades!!* . . . *After supper* when we were all madder than ever with the pulling of crackers, the drink-ing of champagne, and the making of speeches; a universal country dance was proposed—and Forster *seizing me round the waist* whirled me into the thick of it, and *made* me dance!! like a person in the treadmill who must move for-ward or be crushed to death. Once I cried out, "Oh for the

love of Heaven let me go! you are going to dash my brains out against the folding doors!" "Your *brains!!*" he answered, "who cares about their brains *here? Let them go!*"

The party rose "to something not unlike the *rape of the Sabines!*" and then Dickens carried Forster and Thackeray off to his house "'*to finish the night there*' and a *royal* night they would have of it I fancy!" But Jane Carlyle went home and slept— and slept and slept, her first healthy sleep in what felt to her like years. There's some deep reflection in that scene, an image for the age: the mad Victorian extrovert Charles Dickens, his most popular story just finished, gathering up everyone around him and infusing them like puppets with his own Christmas energy. And in it, the mad Victorian introvert Jane Carlyle at last finding peace.

PAUL ELIE

THE LAST CATHOLIC WRITER IN AMERICA?

(From *Books & Culture*)

1

A couple of years ago, when he was still up in Connecticut and some of the priests there were charged with sexually abusing children, Archbishop Edward Egan testified in court that the archdiocese and the church shouldn't be held accountable for the priests' behavior. As far as the church was concerned, he said, the priests were "independent contractors."

When this testimony came to light I happened to be rereading *Death Comes for the Archbishop*. You've probably read it yourself: the story of Archbishop Jean-Marie Latour and his sidekick Father Vaillant, French priests and best friends who come to America and go west to hunt out the "lost Catholics" of the desert and call them back to the faith.

Because the novel is about Catholics, it is easy to forget that the author, Willa Cather, was an Episcopalian. And because it takes place in the nineteenth century, it is easy to forget that it was written in 1925. When we think of American Catholicism circa 1925, we usually think of the Catholic masses: packed city parishes, red-brick schools, armies of nuns, saint's-day parades. But there are no crowd scenes in *Death Comes for the Archbishop*. It is a novel about two men, their faith, and their companionship. The two priests are companions—they live in the same country; they eat the same bread—and their companionship comes to suggest the things that bind them in faith: the body of Christ, the life of the church, the communion of saints.

It would be easy to contrast those two priests with the so-called "independent contractors" of today. But what struck me as I read the novel again was that it is about Catholics who are, in their way, independents. The desert is vast. Other Catholics are few. Rome is far, far away. The priests must live according to their lights. Together, each is essentially solitary. Apart, they are lonely. When Father Vaillant gets an order from Rome to go to the Colorado gold rush, the archbishop is devastated. He passes his nights in the rectory longing for France while his friend goes over the mountains on a specially equipped wagon, big enough for one man to sleep in, with a portable altar hooked to the back of it.

The missionary efforts of the real-life Latours and Vaillants were successful. Today the Catholic Church is the largest church in the United States, and Catholic leaders miss no chance to say so. Yet companionship is sorely lacking. The individual Catholic feels not only independent but—fill in your adjective of choice—alone, lonely, ignored, alienated, solitary, separate, set apart, estranged.

The reasons for this circumstance are best left to other discussions and other experts. What interests me here is how this independence or aloneness affects the Catholic writer.

2

The other day I looked over the books on the shelves in my apartment, and I was struck by how many of them could be classified as "Catholic literature" or "Catholic writing."

There are big histories of Christianity in Europe and of Catholicism in the United States. There are scholarly books about Lourdes and Italian Catholic Harlem, which depict those places as worlds of wonder, where the religion was thicker and richer than it is today. There is a history of the Irish saints that reads like a novel, and a novel about an alcoholic Irish Catholic that reads like the life of a saint.

There is a Catholic's book about how one man—Oskar Schindler—saved Jews from the Holocaust, and another Catholic's book about how one man—Pope Pius XII—failed to save Jews from the Holocaust.

A trilogy on the moral life by a "philosopher's philosopher" who started out as a Marxist in Edinburgh and has wound up a Thomist in Nashville, Tennessee.

A book by a convert who became famous as a naturalist but sees herself as a theologian.

Several slim volumes of poetry, each of them dedicated "to the glory of God."

A big book of "all saints," one for each day, including Galileo and Gandhi as well as Baron von Hugel and Jacques Maritain, and a biography of Thomas More organized around the question posed to the nascent saint at his baptism: "Thomas More, what seekest thou?"

Book-length essays by the best liberal political commentator and the best conservative one, each of them a Catholic in his fashion.

A novel in which four Jesuit priests set out in the year 2019 on a mission of exploration to the planet Rakhat.

And half a shelf of books by the most acclaimed poet in the English language, a Catholic of Belfast. When this poet accepted the Nobel Prize, he described himself in Catholic terms, as a man "bowed to the desk like some monk bowed over his prie-dieu, some dutiful contemplative pivoting his understanding in an attempt to bear his portion of the world." To explain what poetry is, he told the story of St. Kevin, a monk of old, who was kneeling with his arm stretched out when a bird made a nest in the palm of a hand—whereupon he "stayed immobile for hours and days and nights and weeks, holding out his hand until the eggs hatched and the fledgeling grew wings, true to life if subversive of common sense, at the intersection of the natural process and the glimpsed ideal, at one and the same time a signpost and a reminder."

All this variety suggests that Catholic writing abounds and that Catholic writers are thriving. But in my own experience the Catholic writer feels strongly otherwise.

If you are a Catholic writer, you probably know the feeling yourself. It is as though you are the only person left who takes this stuff seriously—the only writer who cares about religion, and the only Catholic who has any literary taste. You are the last Catholic writer in America, and you are afraid the species is dying out. That is one of the reasons you stick around.

Your independence becomes the linchpin of your faith, which is not held or practiced or prayed for so much as it is fostered imaginatively, through your reading and writing and your running conversation with the dead. You feel uncertain, even ashamed, to define yourself as a Catholic writer, but nobody is fighting you over it, so you persist.

And in fact in many ways you are indistinguishable from any other writer. The laptop computer. The grants. The symposia. But you burn interiorly, like one of the French Jesuits of the seventeenth century, the North American martyrs.

You hear that religion is a "hot" category in the publishing world, yet you identify with those martyrs. In theory, they belonged to the church militant, a worldwide multiform communion headquartered in Rome. In fact, "they" were a priest who was alone in the forest trying to translate the Lord's Prayer into Huron in the hope of making himself understood by one of the natives before the others decided to cut out his heart.

3

If the Catholic writer's sense of aloneness is genuine, it seems a remarkable development, since it runs counter to all that we are told we should expect. By most reckonings, there should be a broad and lively Catholic literary culture.

You know the reasons. There are the numbers. Sixty million Catholics—one American in five—and many of them among the most literate and best educated, etc. Then there is the communal character of Catholicism: Here Comes Everybody and all that. Big families, big holiday meals, big crowds outside St. Peter's Basilica on Christmas Eve and Easter Sunday. Mass in thirty-seven different languages. Social salvation. The communion of saints.

And there are our predecessors. The era before this one was a remarkable one for Catholic writing. There were authors who were undoubtedly Catholic and unquestionably literary, who were read, understood, and appreciated by Catholics and everybody else.

So what makes the Catholic writer today feel so fixed in isolation? Why do we feel, each of us, that we are working alone in the dark?

I don't think there is any one answer any more than I think there is one kind of Catholic writer. But there are reasons, and they have to do as much with the nature of writing as with the nature of American Catholicism today. For one thing, much of the rhetoric about the communal character of Catholicism was just a theological stereotype, one half of a textbook comparison with Protestantism. If it was ever true, it is less true each day. And in truth, Catholicism and Protestantism seem to have switched places. The evangelical Protestant megachurch is the successor to the urban Catholic parish where there was something going on at any time of day and all needs could be met. There is nothing more atomized than fifty suburban Catholics loping across the parking lot to fifty parked cars after Mass.

For another thing, if you are going to understand culture you can't go by the numbers. I work for a publisher, and when I get a proposal from an author who says there are sixty million Catholics and every one is a prospective reader of his book, I send it back. "It takes a lot of culture to make a little literature," Henry James said, but there is no guarantee that a lot of culture *will* make a little literature, or that the culture will want to read the literature that does get made.

Twentieth-century American Catholicism gave rise to half a dozen books that will last another century. This brings me to the point I really want to make. It is worth remembering that the great Catholics who wrote those books were independents. They started out alone. They chose solitude. They took trouble to maintain it. They considered their independence fundamental to their writing.

4

I'd like to dwell on that generation a bit. I am writing a book about them, and about our relationship to them, as readers and writers. I would call their era a renaissance—a Renascence—except it was not a rebirth or revival. It was something new under the sun.

Here in the United States were four great Catholic writers at once: Thomas Merton, Dorothy Day, Walker Percy, Flannery O'Connor. (Yes, there were others, and I have had many a friendly argument about which names to add to the list, but concerning these four there is a high degree of consensus.) They knew one another just a little. But they shared aims and strategies to a remarkable degree. They all spoke the same language.

Their work is a kind of "wisdom literature." They were obsessed with the question of what it means to be a human being and how a human being ought to live. Their sense of the human person was Christian, so the question of how to live was, often, how the Christian ought to live.

A friend of theirs had a notion of "the School of the Holy Ghost," and that is what I call them. They had as much in common as the Bloomsbury Group, the Harlem Renaissance, the Inklings, or the New York intellectuals.

But what they had in common is not nearly as important as what made each of them unique. One of them issued a stern warning: "Today there are no good writers, bound even loosely together, who would be so bold as to say that they speak for a generation, or for each other. Today each writer speaks for himself, even though he may not be sure that his work is important enough to justify his doing so."

5

Yes, those four were great. Yet for the Catholic writer their greatness is cold comfort, even a reproach. It compounds your isolation. It suggests what you are not. If you try to identify with them, claim them, write the way they did, it just doesn't work.

Why? One reason, of course, is that the times were different. When you read their books you confront this again and again. Merton's autobiography implied that there was no salvation outside the church. O'Connor asked a priest for permission to read *Madame Bovary*. And here is Dorothy Day, in the confession scene at the beginning of *The Long Loneliness:*

> "Bless me, Father, for I have sinned," is the way you begin.
> "I made my last confession a week ago, and since then . . ."
> Properly, one should say the *Confiteor,* but the priest has no time for that, what with the long lines of penitents on a Saturday night, so you are supposed to say it outside the confessional as you kneel in a pew, or as you stand in line with others.

That might as well be the week after Trent. Times have changed. So has the church.

We don't like to acknowledge it, but what we admire in them is not their books alone but the whole package—the books and the lives all together. We'd like to have them as companions. We'd like to be like them. We'd like to efface ourselves in them, to bury our unbelief in their belief, and in fact many of their readers have lost themselves in this sort of veneration.

But to want to be like them is to miss their point. If there is a single point all their work tends toward, it is this: God wants each of us individually. God calls us one at a time. We are on the same pilgrimage, perhaps, but each of us has to get to the destination. There are no proxies and no rain checks. No matter what church or culture you come from—Catholic or Protestant, in the monastery or on the Bowery—you finally have to believe or disbelieve for yourself.

Day, Merton, and Percy were all converts: the story of their lives is how they embraced the Catholic tradition and made it their own. O'Connor was a so-called "cradle Catholic." But the drama at the heart of her work had to do with the moment when a person accepts or rejects the invitation to an act of faith—the moment of grace, she called it.

6

When somebody asked O'Connor why she wrote about Protestants and not Catholics, she replied that Protestants had more interesting fanatics. If you are a Catholic fanatic, she explained, you disappear into a convent and are heard from no more, whereas if you are a Protestant fanatic "there is no convent for you to join and you go about in the world getting into all sorts of trouble and drawing the wrath of people who don't believe anything much at all down on your head."

Well, today Catholics as well as Protestants are staying away from monasteries in droves. We too go about in the world getting into trouble over matters of faith.

The Catholic writer might wish to identify with O'Connor, who claimed that the Catholic faith was so much second nature to her as to be the light she saw by, and who was confident enough of the truth of "Christian orthodoxy" to speak of her characters as people deprived of the sacraments and the fullness of truth—religious primitives, grotesques, freaks.

But the fact is that the Catholic writer today has less in common with O'Connor than with the primitives and grotesques she wrote about. Think of Hazel Motes, the evangelist in *Wise Blood*. Here is a young man, raised religious, who on the one hand is determined to show that Christ didn't literally redeem him, and who on the other hand would rather establish his own church than tolerate the imperfections, the blasphemies, the profanations of the church that already exists. He doesn't believe in Christ but still thinks the church has betrayed Christ's message. If he had written a book, it would be taught in the divinity schools.

O'Connor explained *Wise Blood* by saying that as far as she was concerned Hazel's virtue consisted in his integrity—in his refusal to let go of God without a struggle. That integrity is the closest thing to a virtue that the Catholic writer has today. This writer still harbors the suspicion that he or she was made in the image of God and that the Catholic tradition has something to say about it. But *what* does it have to say?

In his book on God and the American writer, Alfred Kazin said that Melville "retained faith even if he did not always know what and where and in whom to believe." He added, "An agony in the nineteenth century, wistful confession in the twentieth."

That seems to me a good description of the situation of the Catholic writer in America. The Catholic writer still has confidence in the value of the Catholic tradition—*as a tradition.* Catholicism is interesting. It offers good material. It is a storied history. It is a language we speak. Religiously, however, that confidence doesn't take you very far. And it won't take you very far if you are writing a book, either.

The Catholic writer envies, say, Jewish writers, who seem to have achieved a freedom to write about their tradition as their own without having to agonize over the literal truth of biblical and theological claims.

But our tradition compels us to regard statements about God as true or false. It insists, as Hazel Motes put it, that either Jesus was God or he was a liar. It urges us to look not upon the religious drama of our people but upon the drama of each individual person called to reckon this truth or falsehood—to accept or reject this God in faith.

The religious question of our time is whether religion itself is legitimate. The stumbling block to faith is religion, and even "the faithful" have to ask themselves constantly whether religion is a way to God or stands in the way of God—if God exists. The characteristic believer of our time is a seeker, and what this seeker is seeking is not God so much as a context where God can be sought authentically.

This is especially true of the Catholic writer. The Catholic writer tries to find that place, that context, in the work itself. In my experience there is no better or more excruciating way to find out what you really believe than trying to write about it.

Alice McDermott has said that she doesn't like novels in which Catholicism is a problem. She thinks it should be there in and through and behind everything, informing the way the characters see life and the world around them. I understand what she is getting at, but I think that Alice McDermott is just about the only writer alive who can write that kind of book. In anybody else's hands the Catholic background turns gauzy and sentimental.

I see the situation differently. In my own view, the Catholic writer today is in the same predicament as the person I'll call the characteristic Catholic, and the best Catholic writing will be that which really confronts the problem that, for most of us, Catholicism is.

There are advantages to the Catholic writer's position. The characteristic Catholic feels independent, alone, estranged. Well, the Catholic writer takes independence as a precondition and an opportunity. Most books are written alone, and are still read that way. The Catholic writer, like that Jesuit priest in the forest, hopes to make himself or herself understood to one other only. A single convert will do. The reader must be persuaded personally, one at a time.

The Catholic writer's independence means, too, that this writer can focus on the individual person's struggle with the act of faith. When the life of the church is usually discussed in aggregate and demographically—the bishops, the declining numbers of priests, all the Catholics marrying outside the church; young Catholics, gay Catholics, Hispanic Catholics, disaffected Catholic women—the Catholic writer keeps in mind that every religious person ultimately must accept or reject faith for himself or herself. The best Catholic writing is the writing that honors, and probes, that act of faith.

Sixty million Catholics: sixty million acts of faith. The Archdiocese of Chicago has recently taken out billboard space on the sides of the highways. The billboards say, IF YOU'RE LOOKING FOR A SIGN FROM GOD, THIS IS IT. Well, the Catholic writer is interested in the story of the individual person driving on the Dan Ryan Expressway who sees one of those billboards and really does see it as a sign from God—and, say, winds up becoming a priest. How does that happen? What is that person thinking as he drives by? How does he overcome the bad pun, the shameless manipulation of the pitch, the knowledge that a hundred thousand other motorists have seen the billboard as well, and believe this is what the Lord meant for him?

Traditionally, the doubter is a solitary. We don't read about crowds of doubters. In art, doubting Thomas is set apart from the other apostles. He shows up late for the meal in the upper room where Jesus appears. He gets to the Virgin's bedside just after she dies.

A writer like Flannery O'Connor apparently knew doubt only secondhand and imaginatively. But the Catholic writer today knows doubt firsthand, from the inside. No matter how deep or assured your faith, as a Catholic writer you are perpetually unsettled. You are thrown back to first principles at your desk every morning. Everything must be plumbed, established again on the page. Nothing can be taken for granted.

So it happens that the Catholic writing of our time is often written not out of faith, but out of an aspiration. The act of writing is a kind of act of faith, similar to the act of religious faith but prior to it. The writer is testing the Catholic view of life to see what it looks like and whether it will suffice.

The writer would like for the Catholic religion to be true, indeed yearns for it to be revealed as such. So the writer adopts that point of view, some place between revelation and projection. If it can be made believable in writing, maybe it really can be believed in.

There are consequences to this state of things. It means that there are many sincere books about Catholicism that are bad books—bad writing and bad faith. The writer tries to "correct" Christianity to make it persuasive. The writer unwittingly reduces Christianity to his or her own sense of things. The writer takes the supposedly robust faith of a past age as a subject and supposes that the subject matter makes faith plausible for the reader in the present. Or the writer mistakes a sincere act of inquiry for good writing.

This state of things also means that we can't confidently point to "Catholic writers." A writer will take a run at the act of faith once, then move on to the Civil War or sexual politics. Or a writer, having made a run at the act of faith, will go at it again and again, but the thrill is gone.

It means that there are Catholic books whose Catholic character is not immediately apparent. The successors to the two priests in *Death Comes for the Archbishop* are the two bums in William Kennedy's novel *Ironweed*, companions who hear the dead speak as they dig graves for spare change. The descendant of the Jesuit missionary in the forest is the essayist Richard Rodriguez on a tour of the California missions, a man whose aloneness is as vast as the Americas.

It also means that the authors of the best Catholic writing may not be known to us as Catholics. They may not be Catholics at all.

I think of Denis Johnson, who is known for his book of stories called *Jesus's Son* (the title is taken from the Velvet Underground song "Heroin"). His book *Resuscitation of a Hanged Man* is the best novel I know about the struggle for faith. The hero literally doesn't know whether he is a saint or crazy. He goes to see a priest. It is Provincetown, Massachusetts, and he is wearing a dress. The priest asks him if he has sought help, and the hero says, That's why I'm here, isn't it—a scene that seems to me to say it all about the mismatch between the religious impulse and the church's "resources" for dealing with it.

I think of Richard Bausch, author of a story called "All the

Way in Flagstaff, Arizona." Walter is Catholic—a lapsed one—and the father of five young children. He is also an alcoholic, and at a family picnic he nips at a fifth of Jim Beam while the kids make a hash of the catechism. That night, he chases the kids around the yard—first playfully, then demonically—and his wife tells him she is leaving him. Haunted by memories of his own father, an alcoholic and child abuser, Walter sees a psychologist, but "there is no use talking about childhood drama and dreams: Walter is versed in the canon; his hopes are for something else." And so he finds himself in the back of an empty church in Flagstaff, wondering if he should tell the priest "how he walked out to the very edge of the lawn and turned to look upon the lighted windows of the house, thinking of the people inside, whom he had named and called sons, daughters, wife . . . trembling, shaking as if from a terrific chill, while the dark, the night, came."

A Catholic writer who isn't Catholic? This is not as unorthodox as it might sound. Chesterton's ideal Catholic writer was Charles Dickens. Flannery O'Connor said that "the Catholic novelist doesn't have to be a saint; he doesn't even have to be a Catholic; he does, unfortunately, have to be a novelist."

How else to explain that the best writer about religious life today is a Presbyterian laywoman who has found, in the disdained, uninhabited plains of the Dakotas, a correlative for the experience of monastic life today, and the setting of religious faith?

7

As an independent, the Catholic writer is especially clear on some things. The writer hopes the church will like the work, but doesn't count on it. The writer knows the old language of service and responsibility is provisional. This writer doesn't write on behalf of the church. But this writer also knows that the church doesn't believe on behalf of the writer.

Such a state of things isn't necessarily desirable. Most Catholic writers would like to be fully vested members of the church. That said, it is the situation. Catholics often make a fetish of the ideal. It seems to me that the most important thing is not to posit a shared system of values or yearn for a Catholic literary community that doesn't exist. These things have to be earned, one believer at a time, not simply asserted.

The Catholic writer has to seek a companion in the reader first and foremost. Further companionship isn't strictly necessary. It might even hinder the work Catholic writers are trying to do.

There has been a run of memoirs of Catholic childhood. I'd give a hundred of them for one great memoir of Catholic *adulthood*, and I'd bet that such a book would mean more to the life of the church than a hundred polls.

As Catholics, too, we believe that we are bound together in ways that we do not realize, and that this binding is taking place in ways we cannot see. We are bound to one another, bound back to the dead, and bound to the future in hope in ways that are as yet unknown to us.

Perhaps in the future we shall be a community of writers—or we will be seen as such. But for the time being, the Catholic writer has to make his or her way independently. The work, and the life of faith, depend upon it.

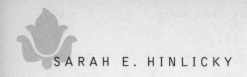

GREAT BEYOND

(From *Christianity Today*)

He just wasn't hungry. It was a magnificent triumph that night when I got him to eat some sautéed chicken and pasta along with his usual bowl of fruit cocktail, but that was a charade for my sake. The meals my aunt Kathy brought down every night were left untouched in the fridge. His previous diet of canned chop suey and ice-cream bars was beginning to look healthy to us; after all, some calories are better than none at all. But no amount of aromatic sausage meatballs or drippy sweet corn on the cob was going to change the fact that he didn't want to live anymore, which was why he didn't want to eat anymore, either. The facts added up, but that doesn't mean they made sense to me.

I'm still too young, I still have too many dreams and delusions, to be ready to die. I tell myself I'm not afraid of death because I trust the promise of the resurrection, but that is a pious lie. Death is the great terrifying beyond, and God (seriously considered) is pretty terrifying too, especially when I realize that death will someday remove the curtain of matter and sin and creation groaning in labor pains that buffer me from his countenance.

Meanwhile, as I live, death is nothing but the heartless divider, separating me from my departed loved ones. So I call it the enemy, the instigator of chaos, the void and abyss and predator and devourer and jaws of hell and eternal pit of nothingness without a single spark of redeeming value—death, the senseless plague.

But my grandpa was ready to die, and for sensible reasons. He was nearly eighty years old. He had lost his wife to malpractice three and a half years before, and his heart had never healed from the break. His health fled after my grandma, leaving arthritis and depression behind, which in turn dragged off my grandpa's vocation as preacher of the Word and administrator of the sacraments.

Funny thing about my grandpa: he retired because he lost one of his legs to circulatory problems, but for the next fifteen years he kept up interim preaching anyway, sometimes spending two years with a congregation. The loss of his leg meant nothing, but the loss of my grandma meant everything; it put him out of the pulpit for good. With no wife left to love and no words left to preach, Grandpa did not see the purpose of remaining alone on this earth. Death was no longer the enemy but the gateway to the beloved.

As death crept closer, it was starting to make some sense to me too. I was insulted by it. Death shouldn't make any sense, I thought, ever. Any talk of good and timely death smacked of euthanasia logic, and I hadn't yet learned to distinguish the two. But life, in an apparent act of conspiracy, was pointing us toward death, almost cheerfully.

It started with the wrongful—and therefore senseless— death of my grandma. The trauma of that death in our family had metamorphosed, not into wrath and faithlessness (as I had originally thought were the only appropriate responses) but tenderness and forgiveness. There were small and subtle mani- festations of this newfound kindness—a kindness that recog- nized our all-too-short time together on this earth—but none was more striking than the suddenly frequent use of the phrase "I love you." These are the most used and abused words in our language, almost suffocated under the multiplicity of meanings they are forced to bear, yet for all that, their effect is stunning. Brothers were saying, "I love you," uncles and aunts were telling nieces and nephews, "I love you." Most of all, Grandpa was telling each of us in our turn, "I love you."

We always knew he loved us. He just had never said it before. Now a conversation never ended without the exchange. Funny how before Grandma had been the one to say these things for him. Now, in the sadness following her death, he drew close to us himself. We loved the closeness. But it meant, in however tiny and unvoiced a way, that there was some sense to Grandma's senseless death. *Is that allowed?* I wondered. Or maybe, *Will I allow it?*

Dangerous Questions

I not only allowed it, I got obsessed with making sense out of everything. I don't know if it was a lack of faith or a surplus of faith that made me do it—in this frustratingly ambiguous world, probably both. I spent the last year visiting my grandpa every couple of months, every time seeing how much worse he was, not eating, not dressing, his cheeks sinking into his face, his hair standing on end so he looked a little like Einstein. He was on best behavior for me too; Uncle Mark and Aunt Kathy saw a lot that I didn't.

Yet in the middle of all of this, unprecedented things were happening. Ever since I'd declared my theology major in college, Grandpa had not failed to alert me at least once per visit to his reservations about "gals" in the ministry. But sometime in that last year, I guess, he'd forgotten that I'm a "gal" and decided the time would be better spent discussing the meaning of the preaching vocation.

His spontaneous sermons were more like Psalms than Leviticus and never neglected, in his grand old Lutheran way, to put Christ and the Cross squarely in the center. And when these recitations were followed by my reservations about me in the ministry, Grandpa, an ex-Jonah himself, took me with him back to the U.S. Navy of World War II, to his early adulthood formed in battle far from the family, to the death of a dear friend, to the witness of a Catholic chaplain—all of which provoked him into seminary to reclaim his sorely tested faith.

He got rotten grades the first year, treating the academic requirements as incidental to his spiritual purpose, and left that summer with no intention of returning. But we all know how that story ends: God always wins. I learned that, after Koine Greek, Grandpa took up Slovak, not Hebrew, knowing already then that he was called to serve the Slovak-American community that had raised him.

His devotion stretched all the way to the homeland; the last decade of his life was spent translating theological works into Slovak for the believers in the old country, deprived of the freedom of faith that their immigrant brothers and sisters had gained.

Is it dangerous to ask if I would have heard any of this if Grandma were still alive and he were not so lonely without her? Is it presumptuous to wonder if his own knowledge of impending death pushed him to tell me all these things? Dare I look into my own heart and ask if I would have visited so much had I not known that our time together was limited? Maybe even asking exposes a skewed perspective. The fact is that I had these things, these times, and these conversations, and in retrospect they make an awful lot of sense.

I felt a weird possessiveness about my grandpa's death because I was the first one to know it was coming. We all knew, vaguely and unhappily, but I really knew. I drove up to visit him in the hospital (a therapeutic rehabilitation, we were told by the staff, nothing serious) right before taking off for the summer. Nobody visited Grandpa for a while because the hospital was so far away. So nobody else had seen him or warned me of what was coming.

Embraced by Yellowed Arms

I walked into the room, looked around for him, didn't even recognize him at first, emaciated and bruised and unkempt as he was. And when I finally recognized him, I knew. *This man is going to die*, my brain screamed, and I didn't know what to do with that. I tried to sit and chat with him, but the nausea was rising and I was starting to faint. I ran from the room on the pretext of needing a drink of water, hurled myself into the chapel, and sobbed as hard as I could for five minutes. Then I picked myself back up again, wiped my nose, and came back to tell Grandpa that I had a cold and that's why my eyes were all red. He accepted it.

We talked about his medications, tubes, and nurses; the Yankees; the cousins; my curriculum at school; plans for the summer; the finer points of Slovak grammar. After an hour he was tired and I couldn't contain my grief much longer, so I left with the promise to return the next day on my way back to school. That night the conversation at Mark and Kathy's was about nothing but Grandpa and how bad it really was. My alarms got the ball rolling to bring him home, to die in peace among his family.

The next day stank of the end. In two weeks I was going across the ocean to Slovakia (to his people, I realized, and therefore to my people too) and not returning for three months. The inexorable process of death was going to take place before my return in September. I put on my brave face. We talked for an hour and then I tried to go quietly and cheerfully. But it didn't work. As the words "Can we have a prayer together?" slipped out of my mouth, so did the entire contents of my tear sacs.

I had never asked that question before. Our family does table prayers and bedtime prayers, but just-because prayers don't happen—and so my asking gave me away, even to myself. The remarkable thing was that Grandpa didn't question the tears. He knew as well as I did why I was crying. It's just that he wasn't frightened by it. He was ready for what I wasn't, and so he had to give the comfort to me.

He opened his arms—his yellowed and bruised, loose and atrophied, tired and dying arms—opened them wide to me. I threw myself down onto his chest, wondering if I might accidentally crack one of his brittle ribs, and he wrapped those dying arms around me. I gripped them. There was something miraculous about them. They were so unlovable, objectively speaking, so ugly and powerless. They looked like death. They pointed to death. They even called out for death. But to me, they were the embodiment of love, love right in the middle of death. I wanted to touch and hold them, to examine their discolored spots, to keep them near because they were telling me that death can't annihilate our love.

His yellow hands stroked my hair, and I started to pray, not very well, not very eloquently, not very coherently. He prayed too, calmly, quietly, humorously even. He said, "Let Sarah be a good conservative theologian for her church," because to my grandpa, "conservative" is the logical equivalent of "confessional and orthodox." I had to giggle through my tears.

But then, a confession and an admission. He prayed, "Lord, I didn't know what to think of this business of letting women be ordained pastors. But I see that you have called my grand-daughter into it, so I think it must be a good thing after all." And there it was, at the very end: the man who had baptized me was now blessing me to carry on his work in the world. It made sense; death was making sense. We said "I love you" about five times, and I left, never expecting to see him again.

In a way I wanted to leave it at that, the perfect goodbye, the two precious hours snatched away before death snatched them all, to have it end there. That would have made sense to me. But the sense had to encompass a lot more than me— there was that big sprawling family of mine that had to be made sense of too. Everything happened pretty fast. In three days I was at my parents' home and bearing the (bad?) news. I heard myself tell my father that his father was dying. I thought of my father being an orphan, that he would soon be only father and not son, that we'd be saying goodbye to him someday too.

By the weekend there was a northward migration of Hinlickys to the Catskills, trekking our way from various points on the eastern seaboard up to the hospital to join together, to take communion in his room together, all of us brought together. Not pretending that death wasn't coming, not denying all sense to the reality of things ending, but finally figuring out how to make it right, how to have a good death.

If any man deserved a good death, it was my grandpa, and if any family needed a good death, it was ours. Our tears were purified from the anger and resentment of my grandma's death; they were turned into praise for a life well lived and love freely given.

There was a wrinkle in my calm, sensible acceptance of my grandpa's death. I had thought about putting off my trip so I could go to the funeral, but finally there was no way of knowing how long I would wait for death. So I went. My grandpa left this earth just as my plane was leaving the North American continent: two hours too late. It was bitter for me. I'd missed my grandma's funeral too, and this felt like a double affront. Everyone else was there to sing him on to glory. I had to put a clamp on my grief and keep it turned off, to the point that it was almost impossible to turn it back on again later.

And yet there's sense in that too. My absence required an explanation to the gathered mourners, and at the wake my dad gave it—and not just an explanation, but a story, the story of my grandpa's blessing on my ministry at the end. If I had been there, the story wouldn't have been told, but the story being told changed minds and moved hearts. Grandpa was still preaching to us from beyond the grave.

And then there was this mysterious fact that I was in Slovakia. It was my grandpa's land, his language, his love, his people served in the American diaspora, his interest that got us back there at all. We each went our way, me to Slovakia and him to heaven, carrying on the love of our family and faith into another generation. The work I was planning to do took on extra meaning, uplifting those people and honoring Grandpa's memory. The timing of it made sense. It all made sense.

This is the sense in God's plan that I still resist because it hurts. There is no resurrection without death, real death. Death, where is thy sting? I see you as the enemy, and you are an enemy because you separate us. But your divisions have been twisted and turned against your will to usher us into the new life and new creation. Death reunited my grandpa to my grandma, and someday all of us to them. Ultimately that is the only thing in this life that really makes sense to me.

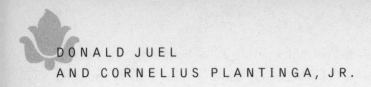

DONALD JUEL
AND CORNELIUS PLANTINGA, JR.

THE UNENDING GOSPEL

(From *Perspectives*)

Trembling and bewildered, the women went out and fled from the
tomb. They said nothing to anyone, because they were afraid.

—Mark 16:8

According to the oldest and best manuscripts, that's the end
of Mark's gospel. Unless his scroll broke, that's where Mark
stopped writing, and early Christian copyists weren't pleased.
So they tried to round off his gospel for him with extra verses
that would feather things out a little better. We understand.
"The women . . . said nothing to anyone because they were
afraid." How do you get a church or a mission out of something like *that*? Where's the Hallelujah Chorus here? Where's
the loud Amen? For that matter, where's Jesus?

Every proper story, said Aristotle, has a beginning, a
middle, and an end. Mark has a beginning and a middle. You
sense that the end is beyond the gospel somehow. It's as if

Mark plays seven tones of the scale and then just waits for us to finish in our heads.

Throughout his gospel Mark has his own way of telling us about Jesus. What he wants to say is that, in Jesus Christ, God is on the loose. God is on the loose and we're never safe from God's liberating power. It's as if Mark says to us: Friends, believe the good news of the gospel: in Jesus Christ, *God is after you.*

So in chapter 1 at Jesus' baptism the heavens tear open and the Holy Spirit descends. Mark is telling us what the human problem is and he's telling us how Jesus is the answer to it. Our problem is not that we keep banging our heads on the glass ceiling as we try to go home to God. Just the opposite. The heavens are torn apart not so that we can get at God, but so that God can get at us! God has to get at us because we're fugitives. We're runaways. We're like Cain or Jonah or the prodigal son, and God is coming after us in the person of Jesus. Nothing can hold Jesus. Nothing can stop him. In chapter 14 Jesus predicts that this will be true even of his death. He says he will rise and that he will go ahead of his disciples into Galilee. He says he will break through death ahead of his disciples.

So the gospel builds momentum until, at last, the big event happens. No question about it; it happens. "A young man, dressed in a white robe," says to faithful women, "He has been raised. He is not here. Go, tell his disciples and Peter that he is going ahead of you to Galilee; there you will see him, just as he told you."

Here's the climax. This is where the momentum takes us. The climax isn't just the resurrection, but also the *news* of the resurrection, which is climactic because all through the gospel Jesus' identity has been partly obscured. Jesus keeps quieting his followers, quieting the demons, speaking in parables that sound like riddles. He doesn't want the full gospel proclaimed till the time is right. "Nothing is hidden, except to be disclosed," but some things are disclosed only at the end.

And so, at last, "Go, tell his disciples and Peter." The young man at the tomb commissions the women as evangelists, but "the women . . . said nothing to anyone, because they were afraid."

How could this be the real end of "the gospel about Jesus Christ, the Son of God"? How could this be the real end of a gospel whose message is that, in Jesus, God has broken through the barriers and gotten into our lives?

Remarkably, the gospel ends *outside* the written end of the gospel. Silence cannot be the last word because, of course, Mark himself tells us what happened at the tomb. He tells us the good news that, of all that has been ripped open, the tomb is the last. The heavens have been ripped open, the temple curtain has been ripped open, the tomb has been ripped open, and God is out. Once more, God is after us.

Of course the very idea is terrifying. If this can happen, anything can happen—and the women know this very well. That's why they are so frightened. We would be too. But all depends on whether God on the loose simply looms at us, or whether God on the loose also loves us.

And the gospel itself gives us a clue in verse 7. Why, after all, does the messenger say, "Go, tell his disciples *and Peter?*" Why Peter, particularly?

Maybe because the unending gospel is a gospel of unending grace, even for preachers who swear that they don't know Jesus.

GARRET KEIZER

WHY WE HATE TEACHERS
Notes on a Noble American Tradition

(From *Harper's*)

> *Glory, glory, alleluia.*
> *Teacher hit me with a ruler.*
> *I knocked her on the bean*
> *With a rotten tangerine,*
> *And she ain't gonna teach no more.*
>
> —"Mine Eyes Have Seen the Glory of the
> Burning of the School" (Traditional)

As soon as I entered first grade, I began throwing up my breakfast every day, Monday through Friday, usually two or three minutes before the school bus came. I do not recall having what are nowadays referred to as "academic difficulties." In fact, I was already the good student I would continue to be right through graduate school. Nor do I recall being picked on in any particular way; that would come later. What I recall is being struck at about the same time as my mother handed me my lunch with an irresistible urge to vomit my breakfast—that, and the sight of my mother on her knees again, wiping up my mess.

I have long since marveled at the way in which my parents, without benefit of formal courses in psychology or any thought of sending me to a psychologist (this was 1959), set about trying to cure me by a psychological stratagem at once desperate, risky, and ingenious. It amounted to the contrivance of an epiphany. One evening they announced that the next day I would not be going to school. Instead, my mother and I would be taking a trip "up country" to see Aunt Em and have a picnic. Aunt Em and her husband were caretakers of a sprawling rural cemetery in which I delighted to play and explore. They lived in a house "as old as George Washington." Propped against one of their porch pillars was an enormous Chiclet-shaped rock, an object of great fascination for me, which they claimed was a petrified dinosaur tooth. There were few places on earth I would rather have gone.

The next morning arrived like an early Christmas. I watched impatiently as my mother packed a lunch for our adventure. Then, just at the time when the school bus would have picked me up, she turned to me and in a tone of poignant resignation said, "Now, you see, Gary, there is nothing wrong with your stomach. You get sick because you don't want to go to school." She handed me my lunch and told me that we were not going to Aunt Em's that day. I did not throw up. I forget whether or not I cried. But, for the most part, I was cured.

I say for the most part because even now, at the age of forty-eight, I am rarely able to walk into any school without feeling something of the same duodenal ominousness that haunted my first days as a student. I doubt I am unique in this, though it does seem like an odd symptom for someone who went to school for almost twenty years, who taught high school for fifteen years after that, who saw his wife through graduate school after she had done the same for him, and who will be in his mid-fifties by the time he has seen his daughter through college. I have spent most of my life "in school," doing homework or correcting it, which means that for much of my life I have either skipped breakfast or eaten it as an act of faith.

And I still catch myself thinking of that aborted trip to Aunt Em's. I picture myself running over the mown graves, past generations of polished monuments, with a cool breeze at my back and the clouds unfolding like angel wings above me. It amounts to a waking dream, with a dream's psychic symbolism, and what I think it means is that I have reconciled myself to death by imagining it as the most sublime form of hooky: the blessed stage at which no one will ever again, in any form whatsoever, make me go to school.

I do not have frightful memories of my first-grade teacher, though my parents have told me she was "stern." I remember her punishing a boy who'd meandered into the girls' bathroom by forcing him to wear a cardboard sign that read I AM A GIRL

TODAY. I remember another boy, a budding Leonardo da Vinci, whose crammed, cluttered desk she would from time to time dump over onto the floor, like an unfaithful wife's wardrobe tossed onto the street. I can still see him kneeling among his precocious drawings and playground-excavated fossils, straightening things up as best as he could, while the rest of us looked on with the dumbstruck fascination of smaller-brained primates. I can see these things clearly, but I do not remember the teacher herself as an ogre. As for the memories of my two classmates, the first of whom would eventually become an outlaw biker and the second of whom probably went on through a long progression of larger and even messier desks, I am not so sure.

Such stories of cruel and unusual punishment probably account at least partially for that hideous strain of American folk humor, with a pedigree that runs from Washington Irving to Garrison Keillor: the Tale of the Teacher We Drove Nuts. I used to know a man who would tell me, in the tone of someone bragging about his first sexual experience, how he and his friends had driven a nun at his Catholic school to a nervous breakdown. "Let's put it this way: she didn't come back the next year." It so happens that I was working as a teacher when I first heard the story. So was the man who told it to me.

It's hard to imagine a parallel from another profession, perhaps some folksy yarn about an undertaker driven to tears by a repeated switcheroo of his embalming fluid and his coffee, a cashier who fell down foaming at the mouth after making change for one too many ten-pound bags of dimes. It's simplistic to say that we see these tales as innocuous because their protagonists are only children. We also see them as innocuous because their victims are only teachers (and usually women). We like to tell these stories, I think, because they requite some primal—as in "primary" school—pain within us.

For many children, going to school amounts to a fall from grace. I have long sensed a mystical connection between the iconic apple on the teacher's desk and the apple Adam ate from the forbidden tree; I am tempted to take them for the same apple. Perhaps the New England Puritans who taught their children the alphabet starting with the A in "Adam's Fall" were playing with the same idea. Although teachers may figure variously in the myth as Eve, the Serpent, or God, they are almost always the flaming cherubim who bar our return to the innocence of early childhood. For better or for worse, a teacher was our first surrogate mother. The wicked stepmother and the fairy godmother are *mothers*, after all, and in the fairy tales of personal history they both tend to have teaching licenses. In other words, the story of our first encounter with school is either the tale of how we betrayed our mothers for a princess or the tale of how they abandoned us to a witch.

And the last chapter mirrors the first: the teacher who took us from our mothers appears in another guise to take our children from us later on. The teacher who is a boy's first crush is also his mother's first rival. Furthermore, in an era when mothers frequently work outside the home, a teacher with the benefit of a shorter day and a longer summer vacation not only spends the best hours of the day with our children, she spends the brightest days of the year with her own. I believe this accounts for much of the disdain for teachers, particularly in working-class communities like mine. If someone gave me the power and the money to make one change that might improve the public perception of teachers, I would give working parents more time with their kids. At the very least, that would remind them to be grateful for the hours their kids are in school.

There are, of course, other ways in which schools represent a psychic fall, and teachers, the guardian angels of its trajectory. Although schools in a democracy purport to exist for the creation of "a level playing field," it does not take us long to discover that level playing fields exist mainly to sort out winners from losers. Unless we came from a large family with parents who went out of their way to play favorites, school was our first introduction to the idea of relative merit. It is not an idea with as much application to the so-called real world as we might think. Neither are any number of schoolhouse rigors justified in that name. Certainly we encounter relative merit in the world. My work as an adult is evaluated and rewarded, and I must face the fact that others are going to be better at it than I am.

But that oppressive sense of minute gradation, of success not as a mansion of many rooms but as a ladder of infinite rungs—where does that exist but in a classroom, or in the imagination of the adult who still sits there? To be a kid again, I must walk to my assigned place in a room ranked with little desks, each occupied by a writer my age, or as he was at my age. And the Updike kid always has his hand up first, and the teacher can't seem to get enough of his stories about rabbits, whereas my poems about turtles always seem to lag behind in her esteem. "Taking your degree" is the most precise phrase in all of education: that is what we take from our first day in kindergarten, our *degree* of relative worth. The educational apple of Adam's Fall, by which the first American primer said "we sinnéd all," did not give us the knowledge of good and evil but of good, better, and best, world without end.

Another way in which our teachers took us out of the Garden was by taking us out of the moment. It was in school that the future first began its incessant bullying of the present and the past. The watchword was "preparation," and, considered only by the criterion of effective pedagogy, the watchword could hardly be called progressive. Ask a random sample of parents if and when school began to grow sour for their kids, and they will usually say, "Sometime around fourth or fifth grade"; that is, when teachers began working with a more intentional zeal to "get kids ready for high school," a process that might be likened to getting Sir John Gielgud ready to do a Pepsi commercial. Diminishment follows diminishment, until we reach graduate school, where the ability and certainly the desire to teach are not only rare but generally held in contempt. Few can go that far without developing grave suspicions about the future—perhaps one reason why so many people end up stalled in graduate school. The Serpent promised that we would become "as gods," though it seems that what he really meant is that with the right amount of training and gumption we could become as serpents.

For some of us that meant we could become teachers. We could bring the process of preparation full circle, like the myth of the serpent that devours its own tail. That is, admittedly, a paradoxical image. To be a teacher in America is to embody any number of seeming contradictions, some peculiar to the profession and others intrinsic to the nature of democracy itself.

For one thing, teachers can find themselves an embarrassing exception to the first article of their own creed: that education prepares one to be privileged and prosperous. Of the professional classes, theirs is probably one of the least esteemed; it is certainly one of the least paid. Teaching has traditionally been a port of entry, the Ellis Island by which the children of blue-collar workers entered the professional classes. I seldom see a first-year teacher with her tote bag or briefcase without conjuring up the image of an immigrant and his duffel bag of worldly belongings—so full of faith, so free of cynicism, so ripe for exploitation. And such an easy target for prejudice.

Occupying a no-man's-land between the union hall and the reserved parking space, able in some cases to take a sabbatical but in many cases unable to get to a toilet, teachers sometimes find themselves caught in a crossfire of contradictory resentments. On the one hand, the public expects teachers to have some of the same expertise and even some of the same polish as physicians, though no teacher of my acquaintance has ever had the opportunity of hiring his own nurse in the form of a classroom aide—assuming he even had one. On the other hand, those who see teachers as no more than a highly specialized class of clock-punchers are prone to ask what truck driver ever had a nine-week vacation, or what waitress ever had a pension fund.

It almost goes without saying that a teacher's perceived status will vary with the status of the perceiver. So to the svelte mom in the Volvo, Ms. Hart is an air-headed twit without a creative bone in her body, who probably had to write crib notes all over her chubby little hand just to get through Hohum State College with a C. To the burly dad in the rusty pickup truck, Ms. Hart is a book-addled flake without a practical bone in her body but with plenty of good teeth in her head thanks to a dental plan that comes out of said dad's property taxes. In Shakespeare's *King Henry VI*, a common rebel known as Dick the Butcher says, "The first thing we do, let's kill all the lawyers," but to honor the sentiments inside as well as outside the palace Ms. Hart has to die first.

Of course there are any number of parents, in Volvos, old Fords, and on Harley-Davidsons, who will see Ms. Hart as an angel. And of those who see otherwise, might at least a few be responding to her pedagogical competence rather than to her professional status? Undoubtedly so. Teachers probably provide some of the most and least inspiring examples we have of human beings in the act of work. A friend of mine remarked to me recently, "No one, not even a farmer, works harder than a hardworking teacher. But there is nothing on this earth lazier than a lazy teacher." Having taught school for a good part of my adult life, I tend to agree. I wouldn't say that extremes of this kind are unique to teachers, however. I would propose that the same extremes can be found in any occupation that shares the following characteristics: a notable degree of specialized training, a mission to help other human beings, a duty to help them irrespective of their ability to pay, and a measure of authority that comes from all of the above. In short, the extremes of character and performance that exist among teachers also exist among doctors and police. But most of us, even if we grow up to be invalids or criminals, will have spent more time with teachers than with either of their counterparts.

What also sets teachers apart is the milder consequences of their extremes. Doctors and cops can kill somebody or save her life; teachers at their worst or best can usually do no more than to ruin or to improve it. Because the extremes of benefit and detriment are less, the mystique may be less also. But because those extremes do exist and are so noticeable, the mediocre quality of the mediocre teacher tends to be noticeable as well. An average guy seldom looks more average than in front of a classroom.

In a society that touts both "excellence" and "equality," teachers are perhaps our best example of the complex interplay of those two values—both in the evaluative nature of their work and in their own status as workers. We put them down in the clichés of populist rhetoric and we put them up in the titanium shrines of space shuttles, but the truth is, taken as a whole, they're probably more representative of "ordinary Americans" than any single occupational group. If I were Arthur Miller, I would not have made Willy Loman a salesman; I would have made him a teacher. In the lines in which Willy calls the Chevrolet "the greatest car ever built" and then, several pages later, says, "That goddamn Chevrolet, they ought to prohibit the manufacture of that car!" I would have him talking about the American public school.

Yet another way in which the conflicting currents of our democracy affect our resentment of teachers has to do with how we conceive of service, which is not much different from how Süleyman the Magnificent conceived of service. In aristocratic societies, service is the butler who appears when the master pulls the velvet bell rope. In a society like ours, service is the desk clerk who's supposed to come running (with a smile) whenever any tourist slaps the bell. Our version may be the more "democratic," but like the Greeks, whose democracies preceded our own, we always seem to need a few slaves in order to feel truly emancipated.

It would be foolish to suggest that teachers are a kind of

slave. It would be equally foolish to forget that not so long ago they were virtually a kind of indentured servant. That they have advanced beyond servitude is not always regarded as a cause for celebration. Add teachers to that list of groups and persons who eventually "got so uppity" that they threatened to diminish the status that came of having them under our thumbs. Here again I must be careful not to overstate my case. One of my favorite school stories has to do with a principal who told a friend of mine that although he understood his frustration when his son's teacher consistently failed to return his phone calls, he should understand that "returning calls has never been Mrs. Van Winkle's strength."

Still, even when one allows for the maddening imperviousness—and equally maddening impunity—of certain teachers, one is still struck from time to time by the popular assumption that public schools, like Third World bazaars and Atlantic City casinos, ought to be places where the almighty spender can throw his weight around like Almighty God. Whenever one hears that dearly beloved phrase "local control," and one hears it in my corner of New England about once a day, the accent is usually on *control,* and the control, firmly on the teachers. Of course this is also true beyond the local level, most recently in proposals to fingerprint teachers in order to "protect children." What politician as keen on protecting his or her career as on protecting children would ever propose fingerprinting clergy, orthodontists, or live-in boyfriends? Not to forget every legislator employing a page.

For the most part, though, I do not hear teachers criticized for having slipped their leashes so much as for having dropped their halos. "Teachers are not supposed to be in it for the money; they're supposed to be in it for the children"—a sentiment that sounds reasonable enough until we remember that even the most altruistic teachers have been known to produce children, and that teachers' children have been known to eat. Still, one can almost hear the aggrieved tones of unrequited love in the voices of those who wistfully recall the days "when a teacher was respected" and wouldn't have known what to do with anything so crass as a dollar bill, not if you taped it to her nose.

Once again there's a contradiction lurking under the rhetoric, which reveals a cultural contradiction as well. Teachers are also resented *for* their altruism, and one does not have to look too far for examples of the resentment. I remember sitting next to a father at Town Meeting who in his litany of grievances against teachers closed with this: "They teach kids not to work." It was a hardworking man who said this. What I think he meant was: "They teach kids that there are other things in life *besides* work, that is, besides work done for money." I recall another father, also hardworking but with the added perspective of being a teacher's husband, who gave as his explanation for the bitter controversy surrounding a guidance counselor at his school: "I think people resent her goodness."

It was a remark that struck home, in part because home for me is a hardscrabble place where many people have led very hard lives. In their eyes, teachers make children unfit to live in a world where survival belongs to the toughest. Special education, cooperative learning, second chances—even art and music—are "fine for some," but what have such things to do with real life as these people have known it? And if all this coddling is indeed valuable, does that mean that a hard life is not? I'm told there's a Sicilian proverb that says, "It's a foolish man who educates his children so they can despise him." It's a foolish man who doesn't see that fear at the root of nearly everything we might call reactionary.

People are said to hate change, even though in our society political change, at least, is supposed to come about by the will of the people. I imagine that for many of them hating teachers comes down to the same thing. Whenever our society changes, or wishes to change, or pretends that it wishes to change, schools and teachers are enlisted in the cause. If we decide that cyberspace is the place to go, we start by sending the second grade. If we come to fear that morality is going to hell in a handbasket, we draw up a curriculum of "values-based" education. No teacher can hear the phrase "launching a new initiative" without knowing that the launching pad is going to be located on top of his desk.

If we oppose a given change, we may be inclined to disdain the teacher who carries it forward, though in many cases this amounts to hearing bad news and killing the messenger. Our chagrin can come not only from the change itself but from the sense of having to subsidize our own obsolescence. We shall never require a sign outside a school building that reads YOUR TAX DOLLARS AT WORK; people feel them at work, no less than the workings of their own bowels, which is why, in times of unsettling social change and political insecurity, citizens will sometimes descend with merciless indignation on a school budget. The first thing we do, let's kill all the special programs. I have even heard people say, "It's the one thing left that I have some control over."

But schools have not only been placed in the vanguard of change; they have in many ways been used to contain and minimize change. So if, for instance, we want to continue to practice de facto racial segregation, we can pretend otherwise by busing children between racially homogeneous schools. If we are content to see the gap between rich and poor grow wider every year, but wish to seem more "compassionate," we can try to establish some semblance of equity in the funding of public education. Ostensibly, our guiding principle here is that the first step in changing society for the better is changing schools.

That is a fairly sound guiding principle—provided that the *first* step doesn't wind up being the *only* step. Schools can indeed be better places than the communities that sustain them, but never much better, and never better for long. In the end, we can only change the world by changing the world. When something happens in a schoolyard to remind us of this, something awful and sad, we lash out at "the teachers" and "the schools." They were supposed to be making the world a better place, or at least maintaining the illusion that we wanted them to.

Public schools embody our democratic principles and contradictions better than any other institution we know. In schools we behold our own spitting image as a people who value equality but crave excellence, who live for the moment but bet on the future, who espouse altruism but esteem self-reliance, who sincerely believe in change but just as sincerely doubt that change will do them any good. Whether we call these contradictions schizophrenia or creative tension, beauty or ugliness, will depend on the eye of the beholder. Public-school teachers themselves are no less an embodiment of the same contradictions, just as in the broadest sense all teachers embody the subjects that they teach. At least the more memorable ones do. Think of it sometime: lean Mr. Silverstein didn't teach you math; he *was* math, fleshed out in its angular glory. All of this is to say that the best teaching is incarnational. Teaching is the *word*—the music, the formula, and even the Constitution of the United States—made flesh and dwelling among us.

The forty-odd years that I have spent in school are not unlike the forty-eight years I have spent in my body, a mix of pain and pleasure in which the pain has perhaps been more intense but the pleasure more constant, more influential, and, in some way I can't entirely explain, more true. At some level it was most fitting that my mother sent me off to school that morning, and every morning, by handing me my lunch, as if to say that the part of me that learns is one with the part that eats, even if on certain mornings it was also one with the part that pukes. In contrast, the daydream of the boy I was at six, playing among the tombstones when he ought to have been at school, amounts to a wish for disembodiment. It is the vision of a gnostic heaven, in which the emancipated spirits of the elect rise from the complications of the flesh, not in a new body but in no body at all.

The same can be said for many of the present initiatives to diminish radically the scope of public education in America, if not to abolish it altogether. The utopian school, the cyber-school, the voucher-subsidized school, the school of "school choice," all reduce to a fantasy of social and political transcendence—an attempt to sidestep the contradictions of democracy, the cruel jokes of genetics, the crueler jokes of class, and the darker side of diversity. If we can but find the right gnosis, you see, the secret path to educational enlightenment, we shall at last be able to shed the blemished, prickly skin of the body politic and live as unencumbered spirits with harps and cornets or whichever golden instrument best accompanies the appropriate lifestyle choice. It may sound like a return to Eden, like the miraculous reversal of some irreversible fall, but make no mistake; it is the equivalent of a wish for death.

RICHARD LISCHER

OPEN SECRETS

(From *Leadership*)

On Tuesday morning after my installation as pastor of New Cana Lutheran Church in southern Illinois, not far from St. Louis, Leonard Semanns came by my study to orient me to the community. He brought along the elders, three men charged with the spiritual oversight of the congregation, which in practice amounted to making sure that Sunday services ran on time and that Confirmation instruction was provided. As I would learn in succeeding weeks, they gathered every Sunday in the sacristy for ritual kibitzing before and after each service.

The trustees, on the other hand, were in charge of the church's physical properties. They weren't required to possess the spiritual aptitude of the elders. Unlike the trustees, who were almost always old and retired, and unlike the members of the cemetery committee, who were even older—older than the dirt they supervised—the elders tended to be middle-aged, the sons of trustees.

That morning Leonard and his cousin Gus spread out a hand-drawn map of the parish with each house and farm labeled. Members of the church were marked in red. The two of them, along with elders Bud Jordan and Ronnie Semanns, stood in their overalls in a respectful circle around my desk.

Their running commentary reminded me of a "talking map" I had once seen at the Gettysburg National Battlefield. Press a button near the site of a particular battle, and a recorded voice begins explaining it.

I had been heard to complain that the church kept no roster of its members. How can you organize a church without a list? I wanted to know. With their talking map they were remedying the situation.

"That would be Milfords' place. Him and Clara moved there when his dad quit farming. You want to see a man plow a straight furrow, you watch old Ben." Leonard and Gus exchanged knowing looks like a secret handshake. "You want to see the crookedest furrow in county, then I believe you'd have to visit Martin's place in the spring."

The four laughed uproariously. They were not bothering with last names and may have noticed my confusion. "Milford's Clara and Martin's Clara are both Dullmanns—of the Cherry Grove Dullmanns. Their mothers were cousins. Semanns and Dullmanns have been clost."

"Semanns is the right name for farmers, isn't it," I said. "You know, since it means *seed* in Latin." The four looked at me without expression.

Leonard continued as if I hadn't spoken. "So you can see, Pastor, that every house on the Loop Road belongs to a member."

"What's the blank space behind the church?" I asked.

"That ain't nothin' but the Brush," said Ronnie. "We don't have any members from the Brush. That's mainly Irish and Hoosiers back in there. No church people."

"Hoosiers?"

"You know, Trash," Gus clarified.

"Have we ever had members from the Brush?" I asked. The only non-Semanns in the group, Bud, who worked as a plumber when he wasn't farming, recollected something. "There was one, an immigrant . . ." Then he stopped mysteriously and gave no indication that he would continue anytime soon. I wanted to say, "I thought we were all immigrants on this prairie," but held my tongue.

"Let me ask you about somebody else," I said. "The big man at the reception with the two boys. Where are they on the map?"

"That'd be Buster Toland. He works at the garage. The young'un is Max. Poor Bust owes everybody. And Max, well, he's slow, Pastor, real slow."

"Does Buster have a wife?" The foursome sighed as if about to tell me that I needed a new fuel pump.

"He does," Ronnie said regretfully.

At this point Leonard took command. "That family would have a chance at being a decent family—only a chance, mind you, what with them boys' problems—if they had a woman who was solid. But she ain't. Beulah's on dope."

"Dope!" I exclaimed.

"Yes," he replied adamantly. "I call it dope. She's got every doctor in Alton, Blaydon, and Cherry Grove prescribing her pills. And Medicare pays. You and I pay!"

The subject was getting reframed in a hurry, so I asked again, "Where are they on the map?"

"Next to Buford's Garage where Buster works."

"I don't see a house for them."

"They're renters."

Wonder, Bread

My first week brought a tumble of pastoral duties. Although I had yet to preach my first sermon or celebrate my first public Eucharist, I brought communion to one of my parishioners in the hospital. His name was Alfred.

Alfred and I had the place pretty much to ourselves as I prepared for the momentous event of my first Eucharist. Only the community rightly celebrates communion and when private distribution is necessary, the pastor should bring the consecrated elements from the community's Sunday meal. But Alfred was sick, dying, and through his daughters and son he had asked for the Eucharist. He apparently didn't mind that it was a stranger who would bring him the Bread of Life.

I brought my kit, which included a tiny paten and a screw-together chalice, a seminary graduation gift. We made the confession and absolution together and recited Psalm 46, "God is our refuge and strength, a very present help in trouble." His gruff voice betrayed no emotion as he recited the words, which he uttered like a man breaking rocks with a sledge.

We were making Eucharist on a hospital tray on wheels. I poured some wine into my little chalice and set it before him, but when I reached farther into the kit I discovered to my horror that I had forgotten the wafers. "I don't have any bread," I said. Then, as if he were dead as well as dying, I repeated myself more loudly, *"No bread."*

Alfred looked deeply into my face and sighed. His eyes quickly surveyed the ward, as mine had done a split-second earlier, in hopes of spotting a stray scrap of bread on a lunch tray. No such luck. "Well, why don't you get some bread . . . Pastor." He stressed the last word of the sentence in order to remind me of something about me. "I'll be here."

The hospital kitchen was closed until 5:00 P.M., so I drove into town and sped back to the hospital and entered as though nothing had happened.

Take eat. This is my body given in death for you, I said for the first time in my life. Receive this host. Jesus is the host at every sacramental meal, no matter if it is celebrated at the high altar of a great cathedral or in the deserted ward of a country hospital. Jesus hosted our little meal, too, and did not forsake Alfred. I was his stand-in on this bleak occasion, but I had proved less than hospitable. With ten years of theology under my belt, I had scrambled awkwardly to produce a scrap of God's body for a dying man.

Barely Beloved

One of Billy Semann's daughters was waiting for the new pastor. She was ready to have a proper wedding. This word was only relayed to me by telephone, as Billy himself, who was perennially between jobs and wives and lived alone in a camper east of Prairieview, had had nothing to do with the church ever since someone from Cana had asked him for a financial pledge. That had been fourteen years ago.

"The church is only interested in my money," he had complained, implying that this church, like all the rest of them, was preying on his vast wealth in order, say, to build a marble campanile in the parking lot or to support the voluptuous lifestyle of a missionary in East St. Louis.

According to the grapevine, the previous pastor had offended him by saying, "Billy, you don't *have* any money. What would we want with you?"

The daughter and her intended arrived at the parsonage promptly at five, he having taken off a few minutes early from his job as an asphalt man on the county's roads. Leeta and Shane were seventeen and eighteen years old, respectively.

She was darkly, even beautifully, beetle-browed, a feature that lent determination to her young face from the first hello. Shane was a serious sort of young man with close-set eyes and hair that was already thinning on top. Thirty seconds into the interview, she seemed strong, he seemed weak. Together, they were so nervous that they couldn't even slouch. Teenagers simply do not sit as straight as those two were sitting in front of my desk.

"Shane and I want to get married, and Shane wants to take adult instructions, don't you, hon? I'd come with him every time. I promise," she said to Shane, and smiled sweetly at both of us. "We want to do everything right. Same goes for Shane's baptism. We won't wait forever to have that done, will we, hon? We could start studying up on the baptism anytime soon."

Then she opened her pea coat to reveal what I'd known was in there the moment she'd entered the room, a little Semanns about six months along. Leeta's white polyester shift was awkwardly high on her legs and tight across the midriff.

Leeta and Shane had come to rehab what little they had of a past and to begin a new future. They wanted to get off on the right foot—two poor, uneducated teenagers, one of them pregnant, the other unbaptized, both of them scared and excited at the same time. It appeared I could combine premarital counseling with adult membership instruction along with some lessons in baptism.

These two would be the first beneficiaries of several semesters of training in pastoral care and counseling.

"My practice is to meet at least six times with the couple before marriage, so that we can go over the service and discuss all the issues pertinent to Christian marriage. We'll do a modified version of the Meyers-Briggs Personality Inventory. At the rehearsal . . ."

Why I said "my practice" I have no idea, since I had never performed a marriage, had no "practice," and did not understand the futility of trying to prepare anybody for marriage, let alone two teenagers:

You can't imagine this, Shane and Leeta, but let me tell you a little about your future: at twenty-eight, Shane is drinking eight or ten beers a day and already daydreaming about retiring from his job on the second shift at the glassworks. Leeta is so exhausted from caring for a little boy with cystic fibrosis that she is making desperate plans. Your parents are all dead, including Billy, who got drunk and burned up in his camper one night. You two don't say grace at meals, or kiss each other good morning, good night, or good-bye. You do not engage in the ritual tendernesses that make an ordinary day endurable. And did I mention that Leeta thinks she's pregnant again, and is seriously considering a trip to Chicago where something can be done about it? Yes, let wise Pastor Lischer prepare you for married life.

Leeta stood up in front of the desk and gave me a smile, as if to say, "I have news for you." (She really *was* determined.) "Honey, give the pastor the license."

Shane and I stood up, as two men will do when they are about to close a business deal or fight a duel. In a voice that a boy might use when asking a girl's father for her hand, he said, "Could you do it tonight? This here's the license. We done passed the blood test with fly'n colors, didn't we, babe? We can't wait no longer, Pastor. It's time."

I felt years of training slipping away from me in a matter of minutes as I agreed to the "wedding." All my pastoral actions were occurring outside the lines and away from the sanctuary—an unauthorized Eucharist in a hospital, a pickup wedding in my house. I invited them to walk over to the church, but they politely but firmly declined on the tacit grounds of their own unworthiness.

"Witnesses," I said, "we must have witnesses," again with no earthly idea of the truth or falsity of the statement. I walked down the short hall to the kitchen where my own pregnant wife was fixing supper with Sarah wrapped around one of her legs.

"I need you," I said.

Soon our little tableau was in place. Leeta and Shane stood before me, Tracy at Leeta's side, our Sarah gazing in from the doorway.

The bride, six months pregnant, in her white Venture Mart shift, looked dark-eyed and radiant. The matron of honor, eight and a half months pregnant, in a Carnaby Street mini-maternity dress, nervously brushed her long blond hair away from her face. The women were smiling and blooming with life; the men were trying not to make a mistake. The groom appeared pale but steady, a little moist beneath the nose. The minister was wearing bell-bottomed corduroys and a wool sweater over which he had draped a white stole. He kept his eyes in his book. To an outsider peering through the window, the scene might have been borrowed from a French farce or a Monty Python skit.

At the book-appointed time, I laid the stole across Leeta and Shane's clutched hands and onto her belly, read the right words, and the deed was done. Shane and Leeta got themselves married.

They left in a rusted El Camino, seated well apart from one another like an old married couple. They looked sad beyond knowing.

Early Morning at OR

Two nights later in that same interminable week the telephone range at about 3:00 A.M. "Pastor," the voice on the other end said, pronouncing it *Pestur*, "Ed Franco. My Doral is here in St. Joe's. Gall bladder's rupturin'. It ain't good. It ain't good at all. We're goin' to have surgery in thirty, forty minutes. We need you here—if you can."

"Of course," I said. "St. Joe's?" Did I understand the difference between the Front Way and the Back Way out of town, he asked. I didn't and he explained. He gave me clear directions from the driveway of the parsonage over the Back Way to the hard road, then to 140 directly into Upper Alton and to St. Joseph's Hospital.

I was into my clerical gear and out of the house in five minutes.

The leafless trees along the canopied Back Way were dripping with fog and deep darkness. I caught only glimpses of the Davidson place and the Gunthers' peeling outbuildings as I flew by. An ancient haying machine was eerily back-lit by the Gunthers' security light, propane tanks stood awkwardly like foals on skinny struts. But in the night and fog everything had become strange to me again. A time for goblins to shriek out of the forest. As I slowed near the Felders' curve an enormous German shepherd roared out of nowhere and scared the hell out of me. I felt like a spy or an astronaut on a dangerous mission. Of course, if it was dangerous, it was only because I was driving like a maniac on unfamiliar roads, and my mind was racing with yet another *adventure in ministry*.

At three-thirty in the morning one does not easily walk into a small-town hospital. The doors were locked, and it appeared that everyone had turned in for the night. This was an unassuming place, more like a neighborhood B&B than a full-service, Ramada-type hospital. My clerical collar finally got me into the building, but by the time I arrived at Doral's room she was nowhere to be found.

I raced down toward the OR, passing through a couple of NO ADMITTANCE doors, and found the Francos strangely alone in a laundry alcove next to the operating room.

The only decoration on the wall was a picture of Joseph the Carpenter with the boy Jesus, who was lighting his father's workplace with a candle. A red fire extinguisher was hung in an arrangement beside the picture.

Doral and her gurney were parked to one side. Ed hovered above her, nervously patting her.

The Francos were a childless, middle-aged couple who never missed a Sunday but were not prominent members of the church, perhaps because Ed not only came from Blaydon but was, according to my Tuesday rundown with Leonard and the elders, of "foreign extraction."

Doral was as thick and bouffant as Ed was skinny and bald. You could feel their love for one another in the shadows of the alcove.

"Are we glad to see you," Ed said, as though I was about to make a difference.

Suddenly I realized that I hadn't brought a little book or any other tools for ministry. I wasn't sure what was expected of me. But I did take a good look at Doral, her hair undone, expressive eyes moving from my face to Ed's and back, her face and arms pasty with sweat. She was the most frightened person I had ever seen.

They looked at me expectantly, but I didn't know what to say. I didn't know the Francos. I must have known people like them in my boyhood congregation. Surely, we had a great deal in common, but at the moment what we had was silence. It was very quiet in the alcove.

What came, finally, was the fragment of a shared script. I said,

The Lord be with you

to which Ed and Doral replied in unison, *And with thy spirit.*

I said, *Lift up your hearts.*

They said, *We lift them up to the Lord.*

And suddenly the Lord himself became as palpable as Ed's love for Doral. What was disheveled and panicky recomposed itself. The Lord assumed his rightful place as Lord of the Alcove, and the three of us wordlessly acknowledged the presence. It was as if Ed and Doral and I had begun humming the same melody from our separate childhoods.

That night the Spirit moved like a gentle breeze among us and created something ineffable and real. We prayed together, then recited the Lord's Prayer; and whatever it was that happened came to an end as quickly as it had begun.

My first week had been a week of signs.

I took the drive home from the hospital at a more leisurely rate of speed, returning via the Front Way through town. A delicate line of pink neon extended across the eastern horizon. Each pasture gently overlapped its neighbor like a becalmed, gray-green sea until the folded pastures met the sky. The town was silhouetted against this dawn with a narrative sweep. At least one light shone in every home place. The little houses, in which the old folks were stealing an extra hour's sleep, remained dark.

Soon I entered my own dark house, slipped into my own bed warmed like an oven by my pregnant wife, and stole an extra hour myself.

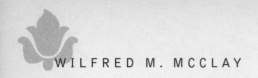

WILFRED M. MCCLAY

CLIO'S MAKESHIFT LABORATORY

(From *First Things*)

The discipline of history is the science of incommensurable things and unrepeatable events. Which is to say, it is no science at all. We had best be clear about that from the outset. This melancholy truth may be a bitter pill to swallow, especially for those zealous modern sensibilities that crave precision more than they covet accuracy. But human affairs, by their very nature, cannot be made to conform to the scientific method—unless, that is, they are first divested of their humanness.

This is not to criticize the scientific method. It is an admirable thing, when used in the right way, for the right purposes. You can simultaneously drop a corpse and a sack of potatoes off the Tower of Pisa, and together they will illustrate a precise law of science. But such an experiment will not tell you much about the spirit that once animated that plummeting corpse—its consciousness, its achievements, its failures, its progeny, its loves and hates, its petty anxieties and large presentiments, its hopes and aspirations, its moments of grace and transcendence. Physics will not tell you who that person was, or about the world within which he lived. All such things will have been edited out, until only mass and acceleration remain.

By such a calculus our bodies may indeed become indistinguishable from sacks of potatoes. But thankfully that is not the calculus of history. You won't get very far into the study of history with such expectations, unless you choose to confine your attention to inherently trivial or boring matters—in which case, studying the past will soon become its own punishment. One could propose it as an iron rule of historical inquiry: there is an inverse proportion between the importance of the question and the precision of the answer. This is, of course, no excuse to be gassy and grandiose in one's thinking, a lapse that in its own way is just as bad as being trivial. Nor does it challenge Pascal's mordant observation that human beings are, in some respects, as much automatons as they are humans. It merely asserts that the genuinely interesting historical questions are irreducibly complex, in ways that exactly mirror the irreducible complexity of the human condition. Any author who asserts otherwise should be read skeptically (and, life being short, as quickly as possible).

Take, for example, one of the most fascinating of these issues: the question of what constitutes greatness in a leader. The word "great" itself implies a comparative judgment. But how do we go about making such comparisons intelligently? There are no quantitative units into which we can translate, and no scales upon which we can weigh, the leadership quotients of Pericles, Julius Caesar, Genghis Khan, Attila, Elizabeth I, Napoleon, Lincoln, Stalin, and Lyndon Johnson. We can and do compare such leaders, however—or others like them, such as the long succession of American Presidents—and learn extremely valuable things in the process. But in doing so, we cannot detach these very different leaders from their contexts, treating them as pure abstractions, ignoring relevant details such as whom they were leading, where they were going, and what they were up against. "Leadership" means nothing if not leadership exercised in very specific circumstances. How does one compare a twentieth-century democratic leader with an absolute monarch or tribal chieftain? Yet what is the point in studying the past if each epoch is to be treated as though sealed unto itself? Comparisons are both irresistible and perilous—and the more interesting they are, the more difficult they are. If made entirely without context, comparisons become meaningless. But if made entirely within context, comparisons become impossible.

There is, then, a certain quixotic absurdity built into the very task historians have taken on. History strives, like all serious thought, for the clarity of abstraction. We would like to make its insights as pure as geometry, and its phrases as effortless as the song warbled by Yeats' golden bird of Byzantium. But its subject matter—the tangled lives of human beings, in their unique capacity to be both subject and object, cause and effect, active and passive, free and situated—forces us to rule out that goal in advance. Modern historians have sworn off forays into the ultimate. It's just not part of their job description anymore. Instead, their generalizations are always generalizations of the middle range, carefully hedged about by messy qualifications and caveats, and weighted down by a certain plodding literal-mindedness.

This can, and does, degenerate into such an obsession with conscientious nuance that modern historians begin to sound like the Prufrocks of the intellectual world—self-henpecked, timid, and bloodless, never daring to eat a peach unless they are certain that they're doing so in proper context. Historians too often are writing for other historians, consumed by the compulsions and nervous tics of the guild, parsing one another's footnotes, thumping the tub for the latest theoretical gimmickry, heedless of the increasingly remote possibility that there might be a lay reader or two listening in on their seminars and catfights, hoping to find words of wisdom and insight. Yet there is something admirable in this professional modesty, however wrapped in self-absorption it may be. It at least preserves something of the genius of history, which is to remind us of our limits and boundaries, and of the knotty problems that are inherent in any act of self-awareness.

History reminds us that our origins linger on in us. It reminds us that we can never entirely remove the incidentals of our time and place, because they are never entirely incidental. At the same time, it reminds us that this has always been true, for all men and women at all times. In other words, it reminds us that historicity is a part of the human condition. Therefore an appreciation of the past cannot be reached by mere introspection, although it probably cannot be reached without it, and without a wide range of lived experience. C. S. Lewis, who was very far from being a relativist, nevertheless warned against the universalizing oversimplifications of what he called the "doctrine of the Unchanging Human Heart," which posits that "the things that separate one age from another are superficial."

> Just as, if we stripped the armor off a medieval knight or the lace off a Caroline courtier, we should find beneath them an anatomy identical with our own, so, it is held, if we strip off from Virgil his Roman imperialism, from Sidney his code of honor, from Lucretius his Epicurean philosophy, and from all who have it their religion, we shall find the Unchanging Human Heart, and on this we are to concentrate.

None of which is to say that those authors are *reducible* to those attributes, so that Virgil becomes *nothing but* Roman imperialism, as the flat-footed historicists of our age might well contend. Nor is it to deny great literature's power to touch chords of universal humanity, a position for which Lewis would be the least likely of spokesman. It is, however, to point out that such universals as are available to us can be apprehended only through careful attention to particulars. They cannot be reduced to neat propositions, neatly ingested. Like everything worthwhile, generalizations must be earned.

And even if they could be neatly codified, they would not stay that way for long. We can never finally reduce what we know about ourselves to a set of inert propositions, because whatever we know about ourselves, or think we know, becomes a part of what we are, at the moment we come to know it. At the very moment we absorb such propositions, we inch beyond their grip. Self-knowledge is, in that sense, constantly transformative. Writing history is even more so, because it means taking ever-moving aim at an ever-moving target with ever-changing eyes, ever-transforming weapons, and ever-protean intentions. "History," writes the Hungarian-American historian John Lukacs, "by its very nature, is 'revisionist,'" because it is "the frequent, and constant, rethinking of the past," an enterprise that, unlike a court of law, "tries its subjects through multiple jeopardy." The past changes, not only because it is constantly growing, but because the things we need from it change too.

The appropriation of this ever-changing past is, then, a paradoxical undertaking. And it becomes progressively more difficult precisely as one becomes more skilled, knowledgeable, and conscientious. Indeed, it is surprisingly easy to write bad history, and even easier to deliver oneself of crude but profound-sounding historical comparisons. It is easy, for example, for any layman to opine portentously about the ominous parallels between the histories of America and Rome, or between America and the Weimar Republic. And so there may be. But it is very difficult for experienced and knowledgeable historians to specify wherein those parallels are to be found— so hard that, these days, they will almost certainly refuse to try, particularly since they have no professional incentive to do so.

It is easy, in short, to treat the past as if it were just an overflowing grab bag of anecdotes, and careful professional historians are right to admonish those who do so. But only partly right. For man does not live by pedantry and careful contextualization alone. Historical insight is irreducibly an act of the constructive imagination, as much as it is a science of careful reconstruction. That will always be true, because the leap from a mountain of carefully compiled data to a compelling narrative or a persuasive theory will always be shrouded in mystery, propelled by the ineffable force of what Michael Polanyi called "tacit knowledge," no matter the discipline in which the leap occurs.

And it will always be true, because the writing of history will always take its bearings from the needs of the present. How, indeed, could it be otherwise? So long as history is still a vital intellectual undertaking, indispensable to our civilized existence, then it will always be proper—and necessary—for us to seek out precedents in the past, and to do so energetically and earnestly, not being content to confine the past to a comfortable imprisonment in its own context. Nothing really has changed since Thucydides penned his *History of the Peloponnesian War*, sustained by the fragile hope that it would be consulted by "those who desire an exact knowledge of the past as a key to the future, which in all probability will repeat or resemble the past." Probabilities aside, it remains true that the past's few precedents are the only clues we have about the likely outcomes for similar endeavors in the present and future. Elusive as it is, the past is all we really have to work with, and all we can genuinely know. Clio's laboratory may be disorderly and makeshift. But it has to be, if it is to remain true to the things it studies.

History, then, is a laboratory of sorts. By the standards of science, it makes for a lousy laboratory. No doubt about that. But it is all we have to work with. It is the only laboratory available to us for assaying the possibilities of our human nature *in a manner consistent with that nature*. Far from disdaining science, we should imitate many of its characteristic dispositions—the fastidious gathering and sifting of evidence, the effort to be dispassionate and even-handed, the openness to alternative hypotheses and explanations, the caution in propounding sweeping generalizations. Although we continue to draw upon history's traditional storytelling methods, we also can use sophisticated analytical models to discover patterns and regularities in individual and collective behavior. We even can call what we are doing "social science" rather than history, if we like.

But we cannot follow the path of science much further than that, if only for one stubborn reason: we cannot devise replicable experiments and still claim to be studying human beings rather than corpses. It is as simple as that. You cannot experiment upon human beings, at least not on the scale required to make history "scientific," and at the same time continue to respect their dignity as human beings. To do otherwise is murdering to dissect. It is not science but history that tells us that this is so. It is not experimental science, but history, that tells us how dreams of a "worker's utopia" gave rise to one of the most corrupt tyrannies of human history, or how civilized, technically competent modern men saw fit to place their fellow men in gas chambers. These are not events that need to be replicated. Instead, they need to be remembered, as pieces of evidence about what civilized men are capable of doing, and perhaps by extension about the kinds of political regimes and moral reasonings that seem likely to unleash—or to inhibit—such moral horrors.

Thankfully, not all of history's lessons are so gruesome. The history of the United States, for example, provides one reason to hope for the continuing improvement of the human estate, and such sober hopefulness is, I believe, reinforced by an honest encounter with the dark side of the American past. Hope is not real and enduring unless it is based upon the truth, rather than the power of positive thinking. The dark side is always an important part of the truth, just as everything that is solid casts a shadow when placed in the light.

Chief among the things history should teach us, especially those of us who live nestled in the comfortable bosom of a prosperous America, is what Henry James called "the imagination of disaster." The study of history can be sobering and shocking, and morally troubling. One does not have to believe in original sin to study it successfully, but it probably helps. By relentlessly placing on display the pervasive crookedness of humanity's timber, history brings us back to earth, equips us to resist the powerful lure of radical expectations, and reminds us of the grimmer possibilities of human nature—possibilities that, for most people living in most times, have not been the least bit imaginary. With such realizations firmly in hand, we are far better equipped to move forward in the right way.

So we work away in Clio's makeshift laboratory, deducing what we can from the patient examination and comparison of singular examples, each deeply rooted in its singular place and moment. From the perspective of science, this is a crazy way to go about things. It is as if we were reduced to making deductions from the fragmentary journal of a mad scientist who constructed haphazard experiments at random and never repeated any of them. But the oddness is unavoidable. It indicates how different is the approach to knowledge afforded by the disciplines we call the humanities, among whose number history should be included. It also explains why the "results" can so often be murky.

There is not a sinister conspiracy behind this. Our professional historians do not, by and large, go out of their way to be obscure or inaccessible. They are hardworking, conscientious, and intelligent people. But their graduate training, their socialization into the profession of historical writing, and the structure of professional rewards and incentives within which they work have so completely focused them upon the needs and folkways of their guild that they find it exceedingly hard to imagine looking beyond them. Their sins are more like those of sheep than those of wolves.

Add to this, however, the fact that, for a small but increasing number of our academic historians, the principal point of studying the past is to demonstrate that all our inherited institutions, beliefs, conventions, and normative values are arbitrary—"social constructions" in the service of power—and therefore without legitimacy or authority. For them, history is useful not because it tells us about the things that made us who we are, but because it releases us from the power of those very things, and thereby confers the promise of boundless possibility. All that has been constructed can presumably be dismantled and reconstructed, and all contemporary customs and usages, being *merely* historical, can be cancelled. In this view, it would be absurd to imagine that the past should have anything to teach us, or the study of the past any purpose beyond the needs of the present. History's principal value, in this view, is not as a glue but as a solvent.

. . .

There is some truth in these assertions. In the first place, scrupulous history cannot be written to please the crowd. And yes, history ought to be an avenue whereby the present escapes from the tutelary influence of the past. But the study and teaching of history ought to be directed not only at the accumulation of historical knowledge and the overturning of myths and legends, but also at the cultivation of a historical consciousness. Which means that history is also an avenue whereby the present can escape, not only from the past, but from the *present*. Historical study ought to enlarge us, deepen us, and draw us out of ourselves, by bringing us into a serious encounter with the strangeness—and the strange familiarity—of a past that is already a part of us.

In drawing us out, it "cultures" us, in all the multiple senses of that word. As such, it is not merely an academic subject or an accumulated body of knowledge, but a discipline formative of the soul. Historians should not forget that they fulfill an important public purpose simply by doing what they do. They do not need to justify themselves by their "practical" contributions to the formulation of public policy. They do their part when they preserve and advance a certain kind of consciousness and memory, traits of character upon which a culture of relentless change and instant erasure has all but declared war. Human beings are by nature remembering creatures, and storymaking creatures. History embraces and affirms those traits, even as it insists upon refining them by the light of truth. To do that alone is to do a great deal, at a time when all the forces seem to be arrayed on the other side.

History cannot do those things, however, unless it continues to be understood as Thucydides understood it, as a search for truth. And that proposition is, so to speak, very much in play. There are two characteristic fallacies that arise when we speak of truth in history, and we should be wary of them both. The first is the confident belief that we can know the past definitively. The second is the resigned conviction that we can never know the past at all. They are, so to speak, the respective fallacies of positivism and skepticism, stripped down to their essences. They are the mirror images of one another. And they are equally wrong.

The first fallacy has lost some of its appeal for academic historians, but rather less with the public. One hears this particular reliance upon the authority of history expressed all the time, and most frequently in sentences that begin, "History teaches us that. . . ." Professional historians and seasoned students, to their credit, tend to cringe at such words. And indeed, it is surprising, and not a little amusing, to see how ready the general public is to believe that history, unlike politics, is an entirely detached, objective, impersonal, and unproblematic undertaking. Not only the unsophisticated make this error. Even the jaded journalists who cover the White House, and the politicians they cover, imagine that the question of a particular President's historical standing will be decided by the impartial "verdict of history." I say surprising and amusing, but such an attitude is also touching, because it betrays such immense naive confidence in the transparency of historical authority. Many people still believe that, in the end, after all has been done and said, History Speaks.

Whatever their folly in so believing, however, it does not justify a movement to the opposite extreme—the dogmatic skepticism and relativism implicit in the second fallacy. That, in its crudest form, is the belief that all opinions are created equal, and since the truth is unknowable and morality is subjective, we all are entitled to think what we wish, and deserve to have our opinions and values respected, so long as we don't insist too strenuously upon their being "true." Such a perspective is not only wrong, because it renders genuine debate and inquiry impossible, it is damaging to the entire historical undertaking.

Truth is the basis of our common world. If we cannot argue constructively about historical truth and untruth, and cannot thereby open ourselves to the possibility of persuasion, then there is no reason for us even to talk. If we cannot believe in the reasonable fixity of words and texts, then there is no reason for us to write. If we cannot believe that an author has something to offer us beyond the mere fact of his or her "situatedness," then there is no reason for us to read. If we cannot believe that there is more to an author, or a book, than political or ideological commitments, then there is no reason for us to listen. If history ever ceases to be the pursuit of truth, then

it will in time become nothing more than self-regarding senti-
mentalism, which in turn masks the sheer will to power, and
the war of all against all.

This description sounds rather dire, but there is no reason to
believe that we have reached such a pass, notwithstanding the
academy's current multitudinous follies. Our actions as readers
and writers of history betray the fact that we continue to
believe in these things implicitly, and would be lost without
them. And not only as readers and writers of history. It cannot
be noted often enough that even high-flying postmodernist
(and post-postmodernist) scholars tend to be notoriously
literal-minded when it comes to the terms of their contracts.
This brute Johnsonian fact offers more of the heft of truth
than the collective oeuvre of all the Gallic savants and their
epigones. Perhaps it does not reflect especially well on us that
we indulge so much patent silliness. It is appalling to think of
how much valuable time and talent is thereby wasted, a
thought that cannot fail to occur to a sensitive soul contem-
plating what happens to bright students entering our top-
flight graduate programs in the humanities. But serious writing
has survived far worse travails, and it will likely survive these
too—simply because it addresses itself to profound human
needs that cannot be willed away. History's tortoise-like resis-
tance to theory may prove to have been one of its saving
graces in a hare-brained era.

Still, we all are better off when we make the effort to acknowledge our actual operating notions and motives—and thereby make them available for rational examination. This need not entail the task of formulating a grand Philosophy of History (too often a grand distraction from actually studying history). It may be enough to remember the two fallacies, which I will for convenience's sake dub the Fallacy of Misplaced Precision and the Fallacy of Misplaced Skepticism, as the extremes we want to avoid. There is a world of difference between saying that there is no truth, and saying that no one is fully in possession of it. Yes, the truth is elusive, and only fleetingly and partially glimpsed outside the mind of God. But it is no folly to believe that the truth *is* there, and that we are drawn by our nature to search endlessly for it. Indeed, the real folly is in claiming otherwise.

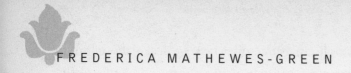

THREE BAD IDEAS FOR WOMEN,
AND WHAT TO DO ABOUT THEM

(From *Touchstone*)

Few book titles have had the sticking power of Richard Weaver's *Ideas Have Consequences*. Even people who have never read it find the blunt title instantly compelling. Weaver's thesis was that the ideas that we absorb about the world, about the way things are or should be, inevitably direct our actions. Though the book was published in 1948, before many current bizarre ideas had fully emerged, the thesis is an eternal one. It sets people to wondering which ideas were the seeds that sprouted our present mess and which new ideas might be helping us out of it—or further in.

Ideas about the nature of life combine in a framework that can go by many names; the word *paradigm*, popular a decade ago, has through overuse become almost as irritating as *chad*. Some call this framework a worldview, mindset, outlook, ideology, cognitive framework, or reality grid; a New Testament term is *phronema*. Whichever term you choose, it means that mental assumptions link together and result in actions—ideas have consequences.

A few decades ago some people got a bad idea. Or perhaps the bad idea got them, and shook and confused them till the right ideas came to look strange. We might trace it to the Supreme Court's *Roe v. Wade* decision in January 1973, but even that document grew out of prior ideas. It didn't stand alone, and it cannot be combated alone. I'd like to explore three interlocking, mutually supporting bad ideas that sprouted during that era, and then look at some ideas about how to fix things.

The Feminist Bloom

It's hard to pin down exactly when these bad ideas sprouted, but I can point to the moment when I first encountered them in bloom. At the time, I thought they were inspiring. I thought I had discovered liberation.

It was September 1970 and I was standing at the public information desk in the Student Union at the University of South Carolina. I was a brand-new freshman, pretty shy, and had been given the advice that I could meet people by joining organizations. So I joined the college paper, and was immediately given an assignment: "Find out what all this stuff is about women's lib."

I was baffled as to how to do that. Feminism had just begun impinging on public consciousness, usually in the form of a joke. It was called "women's lib," and wasn't taken seriously, carrying no more weight than an offhand comment on Johnny Carson about "bra burners." I didn't know how to research the topic, but the editor had a suggestion: go to the Student Union and page "anyone who knows about the women's liberation movement."

I can't imagine what would happen if I went to that same desk and had them make the same announcement today. But thirty years ago I had a short wait, then saw two women coming toward me wearing the fortified expressions of pioneers. Kathy and Rosa steered me into the student lounge, where we sat for a long afternoon while they opened to me the hidden knowledge of women's oppression through the ages. As they expounded this mystic wisdom, I made notes, and nodded. I liked what I was hearing.

I use the language of religious conversion intentionally; just as conversion to Christ confers an entirely new way of looking at life—the *phronema* of the Spirit—feminism offered me a new worldview in a form that was similar to a religion. I had rejected my childhood Christian faith, but feminism offered membership in a parallel enlightened community, one that had sacred writings and advanced leaders able to instruct neophytes in the vision. Initiates met in ritual gatherings— consciousness-raising groups—where we spoke in a vocabulary unique to insiders. We had distinctive clothing and grooming styles, analogous to religious habit and tonsure.

When my first campus byline appeared a week later, it was

over a story that cautiously endorsed the "libbers." I continued my catechesis under Kathy and Rosa, and eventually became a leader and teacher myself, a member of the inner circle and a guru of campus feminism.

A Feminism Revised

This proto-feminism wasn't identical to the feminism of today; the early version was full of energy but unclear on direction, and shooting off in multiple directions at every imaginable target. Not all the ideas prevalent then continued to be part of the movement. Of the ideas that lasted, not all were successful. Of the ideas that were successful, not all were bad.

For example, one idea that died quickly was that women should live in community and pool their children in a cooperative care-taking scheme. This didn't happen because once we started having kids, we discovered that we didn't really like how other people wanted to raise them. We wanted our own separate homes and personal control over child-rearing decisions. Doing it by community vote turned out to be unworkable.

An idea that had tenacity, but didn't succeed, had to do with images of women in advertising. One of my personal crusades in those early feminist days was to oppose the exploitation of women in advertising. I protested that women's bodies were being displayed in ways wholly irrelevant to the products being advertised; they were used simply as sex objects.

Those who think feminists won victory in every cause should turn on the TV or open a magazine and judge what progress this cause has made. This is one battle that mainstream feminism finally abandoned as unwinnable. You can fight City Hall; you can't fight Madison Avenue.

A happier idea was that women should return to more natural standards of physical appearance. You may have forgotten how bizarrely artificial the ideal of female beauty had become in the sixties. Perhaps it had to do with the space race or the fad of modernity, but everywhere women started looking like Jane Fonda in *Barbarella*.

Rent a film from the sixties or early seventies and notice how armored the women's bodies look, how rigid and exaggerated their hourglass figures, how vast and immobile their hair, how surreal their makeup. Remember bright green eyeshadow swabbed up to the eyebrows, and shiny white lipstick? Real women don't look like that; even these women themselves didn't look like that stepping out of the shower. Starlets had to be assembled every day by a squadron of assistants, like a portable tank.

These wallpapered Amazons contrasted with more natural beauties of earlier decades, like Katherine Hepburn or Bette Davis. Likewise, compare a fully armored Ursula Andress of 1965 with Julia Roberts or Sandra Bullock today, and you'll see a real victory for women. Only a few women burned bras, but all of us threw away our girdles, and as a result the world is a friendlier place. The idea that women's natural bodies are beautiful enough was a good idea, and the consequences have been good as well.

Abortion and Unbearable Children

But some ideas were bad, and the greatest producer of grief, of course, was abortion. I lose track of how many millions have died; when it passes 40 million, the mind begins to swim. We can cope with such figures only by ignoring them. Once I heard someone observe that a memorial similar to the Vietnam Veterans Memorial, listing the names of all these babies, would have to stretch for fifty miles. That was many years ago, and it would be many miles longer today. But such a wall cannot exist, because those babies never had a name.

We think of abortion as the defining, litmus-test issue of feminism, but it was not always a significant part of the package. When the feminist bible, *Sisterhood Is Powerful*, was published in 1970, only one portion of one essay focused on abortion. In 1967, when the National Organization for Women met for the first time, abortion and contraception were mentioned only briefly at the end of its "Bill of Rights"; *abortion* appears only as the last word in the document.

Among an array of bubbling ideas, abortion rose to the top, I believe, mostly because it was concrete. How could you measure whether something as foggy as "respect for women" was improving? It was impossibly vague. But repealing a law, or passing a new one, was a tangible goal. You could make a plan to achieve it, then implement and correct the plan, and have something to assess at the end of the day. Legalizing abortion was practical, and as a result it became important. Much the same thing happened in nineteenth-century feminism, as voting rights for women overshadowed all the more indefinite goals. Once the vote was won, in 1920, feminism went into suspended animation for fifty years. It was revived only by the appearance of another practical goal.

There are two other bad ideas from seventies feminism, which combine to create a current situation that makes abortion seem indispensable. Think about it this way: abortion is the solution, so to speak, of the problem of pregnancy. But when, and why, did pregnancy become a problem? Throughout most of human history, pregnancy has been a blessing. New children were welcomed because they built the strength of a family and became the support of a couple's old age. New children meant new life; they meant both personal delight and growth of the tribe.

But for some reason in the late twentieth century, pregnancy came to seem an unbearable burden. It became so unbearable that a fourth of the time it occurred women sought abortion to escape it.

The Seduction of Careerism
Was this because pregnancy had become dangerous to women's health? Was the nation wracked by war or famine?

No, America during this period was the wealthiest, healthiest, most secure and comfortable nation in history. The reason pregnancy became unbearable is due to a twofold change in expectations about women's behavior—two bad ideas. One was the idea that women should place career above child-rearing. The other was that women should be promiscuous.

Both ideas were promoted by the feminist movement, yet there is a profound irony: both ideas are stubbornly contrary to the average woman's deepest inclinations. Both ideas, in fact, were adopted unchanged from the worldview of the folks feminists claimed to hate—male chauvinists.

There is a pop-sociology concept called "imitating the oppressor," which means that when a group emerges to a new identity it tends first to adopt the values of whomever it perceives to be holding power. In this case, it means that feminists presumed that if men wanted something, it must be valuable, so it must be what women want, too. If men wanted to sleep around, women must want the same thing. If men thought the workplace was more important than the home, women must think the same. Whatever "the oppressor" valued was assumed to be intrinsically valuable, and feminists fought for their share.

Take the bad idea that I'm calling "careerism." I don't mean by this that women shouldn't have careers. By "careerism" I mean a half-conscious ideology that holds that the most important thing in life is the prestige conferred by one's employment, and it's as bad for men as it is for women.

This is a foolish notion on many levels, not least because only the most fortunate and elite people get to have careers. Most people just have jobs. When I was a young feminist mouthing off about how I was going to be out in the workplace and not stuck at home, my dad gave me a few wise words that, improbably, sunk in even then. He pointed out that most of the people in the world don't get their fulfillment from the thing that gives them a paycheck. They get their fulfillment from other facets of life: faith, family, hobbies, literature, music. For most people, a job represents only the hours they must spend each week to earn the free hours in which they can do the things they really care about. Careerism is the misguided notion that work trumps everything else.

In another odd twist of history, in the late fifties and early sixties there was a groundswell of concern that careerism was a poison, and too much obsession with the corporate ladder was deadening to the soul. Brows were knit over "the rat race" and "conformity," "the man in the gray flannel suit" and "lives of quiet desperation." Early hippies climbed onto this anxiety and jumped off, recommending that everyone "drop out," get back to the land, make pottery, and eat acorns. The early feminism I knew meshed with that, but within a few years the movement was banging on the glass ceiling demanding to be let in.

In the process, feminists concluded that men were right about everything. If men thought that housewives were dumb, that staying home and raising kids was mindless drudgery, it was so. It didn't matter that our foremothers for generations had found homemaking noble and fulfilling. What did they know?—they were stupid housewives! We were embarrassed by our female ancestors and envied the males. They had power, and we wanted power. We couldn't imagine any success except success in men's terms.

Thus, feminism unconsciously adopted the very values of the people they claimed to be opposing, because it's so easy to get confused about what you really want. We ignored the evidence of our own eyes. We saw men losing their identities in their careers, exhausted from the "rat race," nourishing ulcers at three-martini lunches, and dying early of heart attacks, yet we clawed to gain the same privilege. Even the memory of the absence of our own daddies from our childhood didn't open our eyes. It was the sour grapes principle in reverse: the grapes may look sour, but as long as men wanted them, we'd choke them down.

Playgirls and Biology

Another bad idea was rising at the same time, the idea that it would be fun if everybody had as much sex as possible with as many people as they could. Through the last few decades women have continued to try to convince themselves that this is fun; it's reputed to be fun, it looks like fun on TV, everyone else thinks it's fun, right?

This notion, of course, has been a favorite with men for quite awhile—the last few million years, perhaps. But its formal expression goes back to *Playboy* magazine, when the thesis was dignified with the audacious label "the Playboy philosophy." (Picture the busts in a dusty old library: Socrates, Plato, Aristotle, Hefner.) In the early seventies *Playboy* was a clearly identified enemy of feminism, due to its "exploitative images." That changed; *Playboy* is now an ally of feminism because *Playboy* is such an enthusiastic defender of abortion. I'll leave you to put two and two together on that.

There isn't a venerable history of women celebrating promiscuity; if anything, women's wisdom over the ages taught that emotional security was the precondition for sex being fun, and a wedding ring was the best aphrodisiac. But again, what did stupid old housewives know? Men called them prudish, so that's what they were. Thirty years later women are still going morosely out into the night in dutiful pursuit of fun. And if it's not fun, she presumes, it must be because something is wrong with her.

How did pregnancy become unbearable? Compare the woman operating under these ideas with a woman of her great-grandmother's era, a time when chaste marriage was upheld and mothering was valued. If the modern woman is dutifully promiscuous, a high proportion of her sexual experiences are going to be in a context where the male partner feels no responsibility for a resulting child. Indeed, a pregnancy is likely to seem to him a failure on her part, if not an injustice. Contraception has fostered the ignorant expectation that sex has nothing to do with reproduction, but sometimes raw biology still wins out. This woman may have far fewer pregnancies than great-granny, but any one of them is more likely to seem disastrous.

Likewise, if she has adopted the idea that professional work is more important than child-rearing, pregnancy can seem a disaster to her life plans. The trick of juggling motherhood and career is so difficult that it's still material for magazine cover stories. Thirty years later we're no closer to solving the problem, and I doubt that thirty years more will help. For her great-grandmother, however, it's likely that one more baby would not create a significant burden in a life already accommodating of home and children.

Abortion as Solution

Thus these bad ideas come together, pressing in like the jaws of a vise, and making a woman feel she has no escape but abortion. Feminism sought (1) increased access to public life, and (2) increased sexual freedom. But that participation in public life is significantly complicated by responsibility for children, and uncommitted sexual activity is the most effective means of producing unwanted pregnancies. This dilemma— simultaneous pursuit of behaviors that cause children and that are hampered by children—inevitably finds its resolution on an abortion table.

Feminists defend abortion with desperate passion because the whole shaky structure of their lives depends upon it. Indeed, Justice Blackmun in the *Webster* decision wrote that women had "ordered their lives around" abortion, and the *Casey* decision was based on the assumption that abortion had become a necessary part of the social machine. There's a sad accuracy in that. When something like abortion becomes available, surrounding expectations regarding reproduction and childcare subtly shift to accommodate it, and eventually it appears to be indispensable.

This is why the fight against legal abortion cannot stand alone. If we could padlock all the abortion clinics tomorrow, we'd see the next morning a line 3,200 women long pounding on the doors. We wouldn't have solved the problems that make their pregnancies seem unbearable. We wouldn't have changed the context that normalizes promiscuity and undermines their power to say no. We wouldn't have restored respect for the profession of mothering, or respect for fathering for that matter, so that men would be proud to love the moms and support the children whose lives they begin.

These three interlocking bad ideas—abortion, careerism, and promiscuity—present a complicated picture, and initially a depressing one. If you've ever played the game of pick-up sticks, you know how impossible the task looks at the beginning, when you must gradually and carefully dislodge the first sticks one at a time without collapsing the pile.

Three Good Ideas

Yet pregnancy care centers across the country have been working on these problems for many years now, ever since the first Birthright center was founded in 1965. There are estimated to be 3,000 pregnancy care centers across the nation, in comparison with only a few hundred abortion clinics. Over the years these centers have shifted and enlarged their focus, so the early years' emphasis on the baby grew to encompass the pregnant woman as well, and then both the woman who had already experienced abortion and young people who can be encouraged to make better choices.

These, then, are three good ideas, and these ideas also have consequences. The first is to support the pregnant woman. Pregnancy care centers offer pregnancy tests, maternity clothes, medical referrals, practical advice, spiritual counsel, and many other kinds of aid; recently, many centers have become freestanding medical clinics and provide full prenatal care.

Yet the most important thing pregnancy centers provide will always remain the individual friendship and support that a pregnant woman needs. When I began research for my book, *Real Choices: Listening to Women, Looking for Alternatives to Abortion*, I had the goal of discovering the main reasons women had abortions. I thought that if we could rank-order the problems women faced—material, practical, and financial—we'd be able to address them more effectively.

To my great surprise, I found that these practical forms of support were only secondarily important. Woman after woman told me that the reason she'd had an abortion was that someone she cared about told her she should. The people she needed to lean on for support in a crisis pregnancy, like her boyfriend or mother, didn't supply that support, but instead encouraged her—and sometimes, sadly, coerced her—to have an abortion instead.

While pro-choice advocates present abortion as an act of autonomy, pregnant women experience it rather as a response to abandonment. Pregnancy is the icon of human connectedness, binding a woman to her child and the father of the child. Abortion shatters those connections and leaves her desolate.

Thus, when I asked women, "What would you have needed in order to finish the pregnancy?" repeatedly they told me, "I needed just one person to stand by me." While there are many useful ways centers can support pregnant women, the most important thing they can give is friendship, simple moral support. Across the nation pro-lifers are doing many important things to protect unborn life: making TV commercials, proposing bills in Congress, writing books. But the one thing that can prevent an abortion tomorrow is what women told me they needed: a friend. Individual, personal care for pregnant women is a very, very good idea.

Support and Prevention

A second good idea is that of offering grief-counseling for post-abortion women. You might think that once a woman has had an abortion, it is too late for a pregnancy center to be of any help. The opposite is true. Nearly half of the abortions done each year are done on women who have already had an abortion. In a single year in California, almost 1,700 women had two or three abortions.

Psychologists say the mechanism works like this: A woman has an abortion, but in her heart grieves for her baby, and unconsciously feels obligated to have another to "make up for" the one that was lost. This is called an "atonement baby." But when she "slips up" and becomes pregnant again, she finds she's still in the same bad situation. Circumstances are no more welcoming to a new life than they were before. She has a second abortion, and then has *two* atonement pregnancies to make up. It is vital that trained counselors help women work through their grief and come to a healthy resolution, so this cycle can come to an end.

A third good idea is preventative: to reach young people before they have become sexually active and give the resources and incentive to remain chaste. The best programs address young men as well as young women, and go beyond "just say no" to present the positive aspects of marriage. Some secular programs target girls alone, and counsel abstinence only till high-school graduation, and drill girls to be suspicious of boys and believe they can't be trusted. This, I think, is exactly the wrong approach. If we want strong marriages and healthy two-parent families, we need to reach young men and inspire them with a vision of the nobility of fatherhood. We need to enable boys and girls to behave in admirable ways, deserving of trust, rather than plant further suspicion between the sexes.

The best character education programs build boys into young men who will see in marriage the opportunity to take on a noble, time-honored role. In our culture men are almost continually insulted, and conservatives and pro-lifers are not immune to this infection. Pregnancy care workers can find it easier to send a woman to the welfare office than to explore whether the father of the child might be called on instead. We expect these men to be "bums," and they live down to our expectations.

Pro-Life Hope

Pro-lifers easily speak of God creating new life, ordaining that the woman and unborn child be knit together, and they should recognize that God has appointed a third person in that situation as well. I wince when I hear pro-lifers use euphemisms like "she found herself pregnant"; it sounds Victorian, like "piano limbs." It's as if the woman just discovered the baby in a parking lot. No, she had help with that project. For every "unwanted" pregnancy there is a dad who needs to be challenged to do the right thing, for his own sake as much as his new family's.

Restoring young men to the role of husband and provider is the most important long-term strategy for reducing the need for abortion. If he is there, problems look much less dire. If he is there, she can do it. If she is alone, the struggle is much more steep.

Three bad ideas have intertwined their roots and created an array of bad consequences, with the loss of tens of millions of unborn children only the most bloody result. Destruction of trust between men and women, decline of marriage, rise of sexually transmitted diseases, and other ill effects will remain uncounted until the passage of centuries gives some historian perspective to comprehend the full sweep.

From that perspective, I hope, he will also see the counterforces of health at the moment of their emergence. These forces are there because, like the human body, a human community has an impulse to health.

There are already encouraging signs that younger people, in their teens and twenties, are more pro-life and more pro-chastity than older folks. Membership rolls in pro-choice organizations are graying, while those of pro-life groups are growing younger. At this moment we can see only the beginnings of hope, and not how it will all come about. But someday we will have that eternal perspective, and be able to see how our few and feeble efforts might have prevented some evil from advancing, or even turned it back a few feet. May God give us courage; may he give us encouragement; and may we be brave enough to respond.

GILBERT MEILAENDER

AFTER SEPTEMBER 11

(From *The Christian Century*)

In the terrible terrorist attacks of September 11, thousands of our fellow citizens were buried under the rubble. The rest of us have been buried under the rubble of words that followed. It is hard to criticize such words; all of us utter trivial platitudes in moments when events simply exceed our capacity for reflection and insight. Some words are always appropriate—prayers, for example, for those who have suffered most directly from the attacks. But I confess that, apart from such prayers, I have not been much helped by most of the Christian talk I have heard. Much of it, indeed, has seemed strangely irrelevant, as if we have lost the capacity to bring our theological talk into any serious relation with the world we inhabit. This seeming irrelevance may—as I hope—reflect nothing more than my own narrow range of experience, but there are things Christians ought to say that I myself have not much heard. Each of these points is complicated and arguable. I do not attempt to sort out all their complications here, and I may not have articulated them in the best possible way, but I would be helped by hearing them discussed.

First, Christians should care about justice. In our eagerness to understand what might have motivated Islamic terrorists, in our quite proper desire to remind ourselves that vengeance has been taken out of our private hands (because reserved for God!), we dare not lose the language of justice. What we have experienced is not a tragedy; it is different from the devastation brought by earthquake or flood. When innocent people are killed—and killed deliberately, as is the point of terrorism—those who are guilty ought to be punished. And civil authorities exist by God's providential ordering both to protect their citizens against such attacks in the future and to serve as the agent of God's punitive justice.

We know, of course, that the terrorist networks which threaten us have their own litanies of injustice to recite, going back at least to the destruction of the Ottoman Empire. Some of these complaints are, no doubt, more well grounded than others, but we need not sort them out here. Rather, we must say that to understand all is not to forgive all—only to understand. And what we understand is just this: that terrorists, consumed by sorrow and hatred, do evil and bring guilt upon themselves.

Perhaps, even, though the lines of descent are more complicated than we can trace, we ourselves bear some responsibility for the hatred that consumes them. Then we must make our confession of sin and resolve to do better. But we might usefully return at this time to Reinhold Niebuhr to be reminded that the "equality of sin" we all share does not efface the "inequality of guilt" that also exists. Terrorists have done terribly evil deeds—and will do more if they are not stopped. That guilt must be punished, those possible future deeds thwarted, and civil government exists as God's servant to carry out such tasks. Perhaps we should even learn again not simply to recoil when Calvin says that the magistrate who refuses to bloody his sword dishonors God. In short, unless and until Christians can bring their talk of "reconciliation" and "forgiveness" into some coherent relation with the equally theological language of "justice," that theological talk will be largely idle.

Second, we need to acknowledge that we stand in relationships of special moral responsibility to certain people, such as our fellow citizens. For Christians our final loyalty can never be to any earthly community, and we know that the very greatness of a nation such as ours can all too easily evoke an idolatrous love. Indeed, what we share with Christians scattered throughout the world, even in states hostile to ours, is ultimately more significant than what we share as Americans. Ultimately. But, again, if we are unable to bring those theological truths into any living relationship with bonds of great penultimate importance, our talk is largely idle.

Indeed, if we can find no way to speak of and acknowledge the special ties we have to those who share with us a particular way of life in our communities and nation, then our talk becomes more gnostic than Christian. In the days immediately following September 11 there has, of course, been much talk that affirms these particular bonds, but I have in mind specifically Christian talk. We are good at "embracing the whole human family," but we seem less able to connect that (important) affirmation with the truth that God places us in particular communities to which we have special obligations.

It is inevitable at a time such as this that we should hear much talk about America's greatness. And America is in many respects a very great nation. But America has our loyalty as citizens not because it is great, but because it is the place—and the people—given us. Precisely that is our protection against an idolatrous loyalty. But we cannot have that protection if we are merely citizens of the world or members of the human family—as if we had no location in space and time. Once we have recognized the special obligations that bind us we can go on to remind ourselves that the terrorists have sinned not just against Americans but against humanity. We should hold them responsible on both counts.

Third, Christians need to talk seriously about Islam, for, at least in my judgment, this is a moment in which Islam is being tested. The Christian talk I have heard—and, again, perhaps my range of listening is too narrow—has been almost exclusively concerned to make certain that we not stereotype Arabs, and that we not imagine that these terrorists are genuine representatives of Islamic teaching. Fair enough. That should be said, and I do not think we are in any danger of not having it said—at least among the Christians to whom I have been listening.

But we also stand at the point where Samuel Huntington's "coming clash of civilizations" seems to have arrived with a bang. However many qualifications must also be made, this clash is in many respects between Islamic countries and the Christian West. If our desire to be politically correct is so intense that we cannot say this, think what we really say by our silence. We deny that centuries of Christian faith have had any shaping, transformative impact on the West. We say that our faith is largely irrelevant to the culture it has inhabited for two millennia. Not just words, but the faith itself then seems idle. The influence of Christianity upon our civilization has not always been benign, of course. It has sometimes been bad. But Christian believers have developed a considerable capacity for self-criticism, for criticism of the very communities they love most, and our civilization has been shaped in large measure by that capacity.

Two great civilizations, each formed to a considerable degree by religious belief, now confront each other, and Islam's capacity for such self-criticism, its standing as a great "world religion," is being tested. In order to help us make the distinctions we must make between these terrorists and Islam at its best, we need to hear from Islamic leaders sincere condemnation of the attacks. Not ambiguous comments designed to ward off military reprisal, and not condemnations which—

in the same breath—condemn Israel. We cannot do this for them; they must do it themselves.

Finally, we need to remind ourselves that it is not within our power to make ourselves, our nation, or those we love most "secure." Perhaps we have sometimes forgotten that simple truth of the faith, forgotten how fragile and delicate a flower is our life and our civilization. If so, the terrorist attacks have been a terrible way of reminding us of truths we should have known.

On October 22, 1939, at the Church of St. Mary the Virgin in Oxford, C. S. Lewis preached at evensong. To anxious undergraduates, many of whom would soon face death, and all of whom must have wondered what they were doing studying mathematics or metaphysics at a time when their nation was in mortal peril, Lewis said: "If we had foolish unchristian hopes about human culture, they are now shattered. If we thought we were building up a heaven on earth, if we looked for something that would turn the present world from a place of pilgrimage into a permanent city satisfying the soul of man, we are disillusioned, and not a moment too soon." The threat of war and the possibility of imminent death only magnify what is the permanent condition of human life, and great though the beauty and joy of life often is, there is no security to be found here.

Every time we have some national "tragedy" such as a school shooting we trot out the therapists and counselors who advise us on how to help our children feel secure—so that, I guess, even as children they may live a contented, bourgeois existence. Perhaps Christians need to say something different to their children. "My child, the world is always a dangerous and threatening place where death surrounds us. When I brought you for baptism I acknowledged that I could not possibly guarantee your future. I handed you over to the God who loves you and with whom you are safe in both life and death. There is no security to be found elsewhere, certainly not from me or those like me. Live with courage, therefore, and, if it must be, do not be afraid to die in service of what is good and just."

SCIENCE AND WISDOM

(From *Theology Today*)

According to the biblical traditions, the fear of the Lord is the beginning of wisdom. According to the early Greek philosophers, all knowledge is the fruit of wonder. Do we have to choose between Jerusalem and Athens? Must we decide between the church and the laboratory? Are sciences and humanities two different cultures, or two different windows to reality?

When Galileo wanted to show Jupiter's moons to his theological opponents, they refused to look through his telescope. They believed—as Berthold Brecht put it—that "truth is not to be found in nature, but only in the interpretation of texts." A classical definition of this separation of science and theology was given by Pascal: "If we perceive this distinction clearly, we shall lament the blindness of those who only allow the validity of tradition in physics instead of reason and experiment; we shall be horrified at the error of those who in theology put the arguments of reason in place of the tradition of

Scripture and the Fathers" (*Oeuvres* 2:133). But why does aston-ishment over the world not lead us to the fear of God, and the fear of God not to astonishment over the world?

All Knowledge Is the Fruit of Wonder

In general epistemology, we see how cognition of the same and the similar leads to the re-cognition of what we already know, and to endorsement, whereas knowledge of what is dif-ferent and alien evokes pain over the alteration in our own selves. But how do we come to perceive something new?

The roots of the perception of what is new are not to be found solely in the perceiving subject. They also lie in the object to be perceived. We perceive what shows itself—what "allows itself to be perceived"—and not merely what we want to perceive; therefore, we bring forth of ourselves. Perceptions that lead to knowledge arise in the encounter between the awakened human senses and impressions of the outside world. Encounters of this kind issue in astonishment. If something astonishes us, our senses unfold for the direct reception of the impressions, as flowers turn toward the rising sun; the things or processes perceived penetrate our sensory organs, fresh and unfiltered, like the sun's rays. Impressions quite literally impose themselves on the human being. They im-press us, and we are im-pressed. We still cannot take them in as we say; we are taken aback, taken by storm, and stand there disconcerted at first—disconcerted by our boundless wonder. That is why alarm and amazement are so close to one another.

In wonder, we perceive things for the first time. Astonishment is the source of intuitions. The wondering child still has no concepts with which it can grasp the impressions that crowd in upon it from every side, for it cannot remember anything comparable. It is only the second or third time that memories are formed that allow the impressions to be comprehended, and repeatable attitudes spring up to meet the impressions that crowd in. All our concepts presuppose intuitions. After many repetitions, the child has then already become accustomed to the perception. It is no longer surprised and no longer wonders. It reacts as it is accustomed to do, and as it has learned. That is why grown-ups think of wonder as belonging to the child's eyes, which see the world for the first time. With every child, a new life begins, and every child discovers the world in its own way.

We can go beyond childlike wonder and say, in general, that astonishment always and everywhere accompanies the perception that a phenomenon is unprecedented. Therefore, every new piece of scientific knowledge is called a "discovery" and evokes the astonishment that belongs to something that is "for the first time." Afterward it can be repeated and proved, and in this way it expands the horizon of our knowledge. Yet, we recall "the first time" by giving to the discovery the name of the discoverer, such as the Hubble effect. Because an event of this kind evokes this astonishment over what is new, we talk about dis-coveries, meaning the disclosure of what has been hidden and the perception of what was hitherto unperceived.

Ever since the beginning of the scientific age, we have stressed the active side of these discoveries. People set out on voyages of exploration in unknown continents or "make" such discoveries in the course of their experiments in unknown parts of nature. But every discovery also has its foundation in its objective side. That is why we talk about "phenomena" and say that what has been concealed has "shown itself" to us. That is the passive side of such discoveries. There are experiences that "happen to us." Expected, they yet involuntarily surprise us. If we consider the subjective and the objective side of discoveries made for the first time, we see a consonance between that which has shown itself and that which has been discovered. The dis-covery corresponds to the revelation. We have perceived what it has been "given to us" to know. We have elicited something that we did not invent. The thing is, as we have dis-covered it to be. The world can be known by us human beings. It is accessible to our reason and seems to be determined by a hidden rationality. We humans know more than we need for our survival. Wonder is not evoked only through findings made for the first time. Even if we already know something and are familiar with it, an element of astonishment has to accompany all our knowing, since in the strict sense of the word nothing ever "repeats itself" in the world and in our lives, for time is irreversible.

"No one steps twice into the same river," wrote Heraclitus. What is past never returns, and, consequently, every moment in time is unique. Only that element of wonder within us is able to perceive the uniqueness of all happening, because it comprehends the dissimilarity in everything that is or seems to be similar.

A sense of the uniqueness of every happening has been preserved by people who are able to wonder in the primal— we could also say childlike—sense and can be astonished. They perceive the uniqueness of the present moment with the surprise with which they comprehended the "first-timeness" of the discovery. People who can neither wonder nor be astonished perceive only as a matter of routine, what seems to be always the same, and what they already know. They react in the customary ways they have learned—and they understand nothing. They expect nothing anymore, and life passes them by—or, rather, they pass life by.

Every chance in life is unique. Strictly speaking, there is no such thing as "a second chance," at least not the same chance a second time. We might also call the attention awakened and heightened through astonishment and wonder literally presence of mind. It lets us take the unique opportunity "by the forelock," like the *kairos* in Greek pictures. To live attentively means to be open for surprises and for what is new in every moment. It means experiencing life full of expectation, discovering anew the reality we encounter, and laying ourselves trustfully open to whatever happens to us.

The Fear of the Lord Is the Beginning of Wisdom

We ascribe wonder as the root of knowledge to the child, and to the primal child in every grown-up. What we expect of the old, in contrast, is wisdom. The old are supposed to have become wise through their experience of life and through the approach of death. But, although we undoubtedly assume that one becomes wise through experiences of life and death, this process is not a matter of course. "Sixty years old and not a bit wiser" people once sang in a hit that was a favorite with everyone who wanted to remain "forever young." But how do we become wise?

Wisdom does not spring directly from experience. It is the fruit of the reflective handling of experiences. It is not spontaneous perception that makes us wise; it is the perceiving of the perception. Wisdom is the ethics of knowledge. If we make a conscience out of consciousness, and hence a cognizant of what we do and leave undone, we become wise. We look over our own shoulder, so to speak, and ask: What are you doing? What purpose do your findings serve? What have experiences made of your life? What will remain when you die? Wisdom is a reflective countermovement to spontaneous wonder. The wondering discovery of the world is one thing, wise dealings with these perceptions another.

It is understandable, of course, that we should look for wisdom among the old, but that we should find it there is not a matter of course for all t' at. In order to arrive at reflection about ourselves, about what we know, and about what we do and leave undone, a countervailing force is needed, through which we are brought back to ourselves. This cannot be a particular perception; it must transcend all possible perceptions, and hence the perceivable world as well. In the biblical traditions, the transcendence that brings a person back to oneself is called "the fear of the Lord." This does not mean the awe and terror of the so-called "Wholly Other"; nor does it mean the *mysterium tremendum* of primordial religious experiences. It means the sublimity of God, the immeasurability of God's wisdom, and the fathomless complexity of God's creative Spirit. The fear of God links reverence before the majesty of the "ever greater God" *(Deus semper major)* with a childlike, basic trust in God's immeasurable goodness and curiosity about God's creative activity in the history of the cosmos, the history of life, and personal history. The fear of God does not make people slaves of an unloved Almighty; this fear is merely the other side of the love of God. "To fear the Lord is wisdom's full measure"; "to love God is wisdom" (Sirach 1:16, 14). "The fear of the Lord is glory and exultation, and gladness, and a crown of rejoicing" (Sirach 1:11). It is not a contradiction to the fear of God when "the children of God" in the New Testament say: "There is no fear in love, but perfect love casts out fear" (1 John 4:18). The fear of God and the love of God describe the two sides of God's presence: distance and closeness, sublimity and intimacy.

I think it is important that, in dealing with the perceptions and capacities of the human being, wisdom should begin with the fear of God, not with the fear of death and the annihilating nothingness of death that such fear reflects. We learn from Psalm 90, if we read it in Luther's translation, "to remember that we must die, so that we may become wise" (v. 12). Death merely reveals the irreversibility of time and the irretrievability of every lived moment; it reveals the astonishing uniqueness of life. But this knowledge belongs to wondering perception, not yet to wisdom. In the fear of God we have no need to fear either death or the time of transience, for in that fear we discern the frame of reference for the perceivable world and the knowing of it.

The frame of reference for the perceivable world is its fundamental "knowability." To put it in biblical terms: there is a divine wisdom in all things, and knowledge of it makes human beings wise. "The Lord by wisdom founded the earth" (Proverbs 3:19). The Lord's wisdom is "created before all other things" (Sirach 1:4), and God's spirit of wisdom "has filled the world" (Wisdom 1:7). This basic trust in the wisdom of God, which is presupposed and is spread out before us in the cosmos and in life, can be understood as a prerational postulate of pure reason. Every scientific discovery discovers something of this wise rationality in the world. The structure of the world determined by divine wisdom or the logos of God hastens invitingly ahead of human knowledge, and, yet at the same time, in its divine sublimity it is immeasurable and unfathomable. That is why human beings in their knowledge of the world become not only wise but also humble through the fear of God. "Wisdom is with the humble" (Proverbs 11:2). We become humble when with every expansion of our knowledge we know how little we know, because the expansion of human knowledge is possible in "the broad place" of the sublime divine wisdom.

The frame of reference for human knowledge of the world is to be found in the fear of God and the love of God, because with whatever we know, it is wise to respect the dignity of the known object itself. The person who through her knowledge destroys the part of nature she knows, or who knows it for the purpose of destroying it, is neither wise nor does she know anything. Through the fear of God we draw the living into reverence for life.

Through the fear of God we respect the existence and unique nature of things and do not make ourselves lords over their being or nonbeing, their life or their death. By virtue of the love of God, we love God's hidden wisdom in all things. We see things not just with our own eyes, but with God's eyes too, as they are "there" before God; and we are attentive to the inner side of things, the nature of things *"an sich"* (Immanuel Kant), their essential being that is concealed from us.

The love of God makes us wise, because it teaches us that we only know the truth of things inasmuch as we love them for themselves. Then we do not want to know them so as to possess them for ourselves and exploit them for ourselves, but in order to live with them in the wise, ordered community of creation. We then perceive them in the coherences of the sympathy through which divine Wisdom holds all things together.

This frame of reference for knowledge of the world affects the presupposition, the goal and the "broad place" of the knowable world, but not the methods by which we arrive at secure knowledge. There René Descartes's principle applies: "De omnibus dubitandum est" (everything must be doubted). But this is "methodic" doubt, oriented toward results and having nothing to do with existential despair over the futility of the world, humanity, or ourselves. The very frames of reference that we have named invite us to this methodic doubt, because they inspire confidence that the results of knowing will prevail, contrary to the doubt. Because there is such a thing as assured knowledge, doubt must exclude all sham solutions.

Wisdom and the Ethics of Sciences

The fear of God makes us wise in dealing with the knowledge that has been acquired. This brings into play, parallel to scientific ethics, ethics in the technological handling of scientific findings. It is wise to distinguish between good and evil. It is wise to make out of what we know only that which furthers life and not to further whatever disseminates death. But here we come up against problems between pure research and the applied sciences and in the technological application of discoveries in peace and war.

The first possible conflict—the conflict between pure and applied science—is illustrated by the dilemma in which Albert Einstein involuntarily found himself. His discovery of the principle of relativity in 1907 was, he confessed, "the happiest thought in my life." Its proof through the predicted motion of the planet Mercury in November 1915 convinced him "that nature had spoken to him," as his biographer reports. That was pure knowledge in the literal sense, in a splendid harmony of evidence with what was already known. But then came the discovery of nuclear fission and the possibility of applying it to an atomic bomb, either by the Germans, at Hitler's orders, or by the democratic western powers—a calculated possibility that was already known quite early. Einstein made his decision in 1939, in his famous letter to President Roosevelt.

The Manhattan Project began, and it led to the destruction of Hiroshima and Nagasaki in August 1945, with the death of hundreds of thousands of people in seconds. Pure knowledge and the wondering joy of discovery ended in the raw reality of the conflict of interests and the struggle for power among human beings.

The German chemist and Nobel prizewinner Fritz Haber was faced with a different dilemma. When he discovered how to isolate hydrogen from the atmosphere, he made it possible to produce artificial fertilizers in peacetime, and munitions in war. His research made the German poison-gas attacks in World War I possible in 1917. His motto for solving his dilemma was a simple one: "Whom must I serve?" His answer was: "In peace, humanity; in war, the Fatherland." His love for the Fatherland, however, had its limits. When his "non-Aryan" colleagues were dismissed from his institute in 1933, he sent in his resignation.

Where does the responsibility of scientists for their scientific knowledge—and for what they or other people make of it—begin? How far does responsibility go? If wars between nations become crises of humanity as a whole, and if in these wars the survival or annihilation of humanity itself is at stake, are people not then responsible, not just for the application of the instruments of mass extermination, but already for their actual construction and manufacture too? In 1958, German nuclear physicists accepted this responsibility and refused to cooperate in manufacturing instruments of mass extermination, to the considerable annoyance of a number of politicians. Of course, this responsibility is not just a question for the scientists and technologists involved. It is a problem for the whole of society, for every one of us, and—because it is humanity that is under deadly threat—for humanity as a whole. The community of nations must rebel against its role as the passive object of possible total extermination through ABC (atomic, biological, and chemical) weapons, and it must become an active determining subject of common survival. It is going to do just that or will disappear.

Experiences such as these with the application of scientific knowledge in our own time make us ask: Is there such a thing at all as a disinterested delight in "pure knowledge" of "the knowable world"? Are scientific developments and the financing of scientific research not always preceded by economic and political interests? The first scientific theories of the modern world maintained that the acquisition of power for the purpose of dominating nature was the "knowledge-constitutive interest" prompting the sciences. "Knowledge is power," declared Francis Bacon. Science restores to human beings their sovereignty over nature, the role conferred upon them with their creation in the image of God but lost through sin. Through the sciences, the human being becomes "master and possessor of nature," maintained Descartes in his scientific theory, at about the same time.

If human beings cannot control the power over nature that they acquire through science, they have still not yet learned wisdom. If the conquest of nature—the subjugation of the earth and other created beings—is the goal of scientific and technological civilization, then it is not surprising that all other living things should encounter human beings with fear and trembling. Those who set themselves up to be nature's masters and possessors, and forget that they themselves are merely part of nature, destroy nature and, in the end, annihilate themselves. The harmony between the human side of nature and its other elements gives way to the struggle in which the weaker part is defeated. The community of creation shared by human beings and their "fellow creatures" (as they are termed in the German Animal Protection Act of 1986) is replaced by the exploitation of the fellow creatures who have been subjugated.

The fear of God is a blessing, in that it can free modern men and women from the God-complex that has made them drunk with power and induced the mad illusion that the ascendancy they have acquired over nature makes everything possible. The fear of God can beget the wisdom that lends human beings moral power over their own physical power. We do not have to do everything we are able to do. "Can" does not imply "ought." The power we have acquired can be used for what furthers life, so as to exclude what kills it. Goethe's sorcerer's apprentice had learned from his master the formula for putting the broom into motion but, unfortunately, not the formula for banishing it again to its corner. When shall we learn this second formula of power? The fear of God can ultimately engender the knowledge-constitutive wisdom, which has no desire to dominate its object and take possession of it, but wants to commune with it and live with it in a life-furthering commonwealth.

For four hundred years, science and technology have exploited their seizure of power over nature. We now need another time in which to integrate human civilization in the nature of this planet. Our civilization too is only part of nature. The last fifty years have brought an enormous increase in what we have discovered and know; we now need a still greater increase of wisdom and of wise dealings with our knowledge. If humanity is to have a future at all, that future belongs not to knowledge but to wisdom; for "wisdom gives life to the one who possesses it" (Ecclesiastes 7:12).

A Common Hope in the Future of the Earth

What kind of future can we expect from the scientific-technological civilization? Where are human purposes and goals?

The Industrial Revolution awakened the motivating and mobilizing faith in progress in all areas of life. Today, however, we no longer need such a "faith" and should also no longer criticize it because, according to the principle of competition, every science and technology is damned to accelerating progress continually. Whoever does not develop is already lost. Our progress is caught in the "acceleration trap."

It makes little sense to criticize progress as such; it does make sense, however, to question its goals, to correct its course, when desirable. Progress as such is only a means of reaching a purpose, but it does not define what purposes are humane. We still measure progress according to the growth of power—technological, economic, financial, and military power. Power itself, however, is not a humane goal, it is only an accumulation of means used to reach humane goals. Every year we are better equipped to attain what we want—but what is it that we really want?

Most of the large-scale scientific and technological projects did not develop through a democratic decision of the will of the people, but rather against the will of the people. In Germany, there was no democratic decision to build nuclear power plants. Today there is no democratic discussion about genetically altered food.

Since the end of the east-west conflict in 1989, progress
has been called globalization. As with progress, globalization
is only a means to an end, not a humane end in itself. So far,
obviously, it is only about domination, exploitation, and the
marketing of natural resources. Fewer and fewer, but also
larger and larger "global players" divide this business. If, however, short-term profits should happen not to lead to long-
term bankruptcy of humanity or to the collapse of the
earth-system, then we should begin with public discussions
about the humane goals and purposes of globalization.

In order to avoid the destruction of the earth-system
through ruthless exploitation, it is good to concentrate on the
"integrity of creation" and the "protection of the environment"
and to protect life through bioethical agreements. But this
conservative ethics is always coming a few minutes too late. It
is better to develop a new model for the humane goals and
purposes of globalization and to examine the meaning and
meaninglessness of progress. We have such a model. It can be
found in the unpretentious and—outside of church circles—
heretofore unknown concept of ecumene.

The Greek word *oikoumenē* means "the whole inhabited circle of the earth." From this idea, we can move to the goal of a
"habitable earth" and a humankind to be indigenized in this
earth-system. The household of the earth should be prepared
to give a home and a function for the human race as well as it
has given home and function for the whole of the other
species. "Every ant knows the formula of its ant-hill, every bee

knows the formula of its beehive. They know it in their own way, not in our way. Only humankind does not know its formula," said Dostoevsky. If there is a humane goal for the progress and globalization of power, it must be this indigenization of human beings in the earth-system. For the earth can survive without human beings and did so for millions of years. Human beings cannot live without the earth, however, because it is out of earth that we are taken, and we shall return to the earth. Human beings are dependent on the earth-system, but the earth-system is not dependent on humans. It follows from this that human civilization must be integrated into the earth-system, and not the opposite, where nature is subjugated by human domination.

Only strangers exploit nature, denude forests, fish out the seas, and then, like nomads, move on. The inhabitants of those regions, however, will defend the livability of the land, sea, and air. Many conflicts between economic and ecological interests today are conflicts between foreign corporations and inhabitants of the regions. What is the attitude of humanity as a whole toward nature: Are we strangers or inhabitants?

The always further-developing scientific and technological potential of humanity need not be employed in a destructive battle for power but can also be used for the sustainable livability of the earth. Then this perishable world is not only protected but further developed toward its goal, which is given with the creation and the appearance of the human race on this earth. This earth-system is destined to become the "common home" of all the earth-creatures and shall become home for the community of all the living beings.

In this respect, we should also remember that this life-system of the blue planet is not our property, but property of its creator. The earth is God's property (Psalm 24), because the earth shall become the home of God also: "on earth as it is in heaven."

When the Eternal One comes to dwell on the earth, then the earth will become the "temple" of God, and the restless God of hope and history will come to God's "rest." This is the great biblical—Jewish and Christian—vision for the earth. It is the final promise: "See, the home of God is among the mortals. He will dwell with them; they will be his peoples" (Revelation 21:3). If this final "Shekinah" (cosmic indwelling of God) is the divine future of the earth, then we must already, here and now, deal with the earth as the "temple of God" and keep all earth-creatures holy. We are not "lords and owners" of the earth but perhaps, one day, the priests of the earth, representing God before the earth and the earth before God, until we "see and taste" God's presence in all things, perceive all things in the coming glory of God, and join the cosmic praise of God.

"SALVATION IS FROM THE JEWS"

(From *First Things*)

The Samaritan woman said, "Sir, I perceive that you are a prophet. Our fathers worshiped on this mountain; and you say that in Jerusalem is the place where men ought to worship." Jesus responded, "Woman, believe me, the hour is coming when neither on this mountain nor in Jerusalem will you worship the Father. You worship what you do not know; we worship what we know, for salvation is from the Jews."

(John 4:19–22)

Despite its suggestive power, the striking statement of Jesus that salvation is from the Jews is seldom encountered in the now voluminous literature on the Jewish-Christian dialogue. The reason may be that the exchange is entangled in another dispute about supersessionism between religious communities, a dispute entirely apart from the Jewish-Christian relationship. It will be remembered that the Samaritans—the *shamerim*, which means "observant"—claimed to be the true Israel who remained loyal to Yahweh when Eli allegedly seduced his brethren into constructing the apostate shrine at Shiloh instead of at God's chosen mountain, Gerizim, as recounted in 1 Samuel 1. After the fourth-century schism, Jews forbade Samaritans to make offerings in Jerusalem, to buy unmovable property, and to marry or circumcise a Jew. As John the Evangelist writes, "For Jews have no dealings with Samaritans." In short, Jerusalem Judaism had definitively superseded the cult of Gerizim. Thus the exchange with the Samaritan woman at Jacob's well may be something of an embarrassment in a Jewish-Christian dialogue that is centrally concerned with the question of supersessionism.

Or it may be that in the Jewish-Christian dialogue there is little reference to the statement that salvation is from the Jews because the dialogue is not centrally concerned with the question of salvation. In any event, our passage has not been treated kindly by Christian commentators. A recent ecumenical Christian commentary on the passage says that Jesus is acknowledging that "God's salvation to humanity came historically through the Jews as a point of departure, not as origin or source. Salvation comes only from God." "A point of departure"—it has a dismissive ring to it, almost as though Jews and Judaism are, for Christians, a dispensable accident of history.

Rudolf Bultmann, in a footnote in his commentary on John, gives our passage even shorter shrift. It is, he says, "completely or partially an editorial gloss," since the statement that salvation is from the Jews is "impossible in John [who] does not regard the Jews as God's chosen and saved people." "It is hard to see," he writes, "how the Johannine Jesus, who constantly disassociates himself from the Jews, could have made such a statement." An interesting question that Bultmann does not address is why a later editor, presumably at a time when the lines between Jews and Christians had hardened, would have inserted such a statement. It seems improbable that an editor was trying to rectify what Bultmann views as the anti-Jewish bias of Jesus. It is more likely, I think, that Jesus said what he is said to have said, and that Bultmann's view reflects his difficulty, and the difficulty of too many other Christians, in coming to terms with the Jewishness of Jesus, and of Christianity.

There is another reason for the neglect of this saying of Jesus. In some circles today, it is the accepted wisdom that the Fourth Gospel is impossibly anti-Judaic and even, it is anachronistically said, anti-Semitic. John therefore should have no place in our reflections, and certainly not in Jewish-Christian dialogue. Thus do we with our putatively superior wisdom nullify the normativity of the sacred text. Nothing so powerfully testifies to the Jewishness of John's Gospel as its vigorous, and sometimes disconcertingly aggressive, contention against opposing Messianic expectations held by other Jews.

In his 1955 commentary on John, the estimable C. K. Barrett offers what may be taken as a more conventional supersessionist understanding of these words of Jesus: "The saying does not mean that Jews as such are inevitably saved, but rather that the election of Israel to a true knowledge of God was in order that, at the time appointed by God, salvation might proceed from Israel to the world, and Israel's own unique privilege be thereby dissolved. . . . This eschatological salvation is in the person of Jesus in process of realization and the Jews are losing their position to the Church."

St. Augustine, as we might expect, treats the passage more imaginatively. Samaritans were "aliens" to the Jews, he notes, and so it is that the woman at the well is a type of the Church, which "was to come of the Gentiles, an alien from the race of the Jews." Thus the Jewish supersession of the Samaritans is reversed by the Samaritan identification with the Church that supersedes the Jews. Of our passage Augustine says, "A great thing has he attributed to the Jews," but then he immediately adds, "but do not understand him to mean those spurious Jews [who rejected the Christ]." Citing Ephesians 2, he says that Samaritans and Gentiles were strangers and foreigners to the covenants of God. When Jesus says, "We worship what we know," he is speaking "in the person of the Jews, but not of all Jews, not of reprobate Jews, but of such as were the apostles, as were the prophets." Citing Romans 11, he notes that "God has not rejected His people whom He foreknew," but by "His people" Augustine means only those Jews who are reconciled with the former aliens in Christ and his Church.

"Salvation is from the Jews." Few thinkers have pondered that idea, if not that specific passage, more deeply than Franz

Rosenzweig (1886–1929), who was, as it were, reconverted to Judaism after a very close brush with becoming a Christian. Rosenzweig's view is frequently, if too simply, summarized in the proposition that Christianity is Judaism for the Gentiles. Moreover, Rosenzweig was centrally concerned with salvation, as is evident in the title of his major work, *The Star of Redemption.* This touches on a perduring, and perhaps necessary, ambivalence in Jewish attitudes toward Christians and Christianity. In the historic statement of November 2000, *Dabru Emet* ("Speak the Truth"), signed by almost two hundred notable Jewish scholars, it is said that "through Christianity hundreds of millions of people have entered into relationship with the God of Israel." Then, toward the end of *Dabru Emet,* it is said: "We respect Christianity as a faith that originated within Judaism and that still has significant contacts with it. We do not see it as an extension of Judaism. Only if we cherish our own traditions can we pursue this relationship with integrity."

Yet it would seem that, if through Christianity hundreds of millions of people have entered into relationship with the God of Israel, Christianity must be, in some important sense, an extension of Judaism. Moreover, *Dabru Emet* makes clear that this relationship is one of worshiping "the God of Abraham, Isaac, and Jacob," underscoring that the God of Israel is not separable from the people of Israel. It follows that to be in relationship with the God of Israel is to be in relationship with the people of Israel. As is well known, in the documents of the

Second Vatican Council, a favored phrase for the Church is the People of God. There is no plural for the people of God. Certainly there are distinct traditions that must be cherished and respected, but one may suggest that they are traditions within the one tradition, the one story, of salvation. That story is nothing less than, in Robert Jenson's happy phrase, "the story of the world."

Our distinct traditions reflect differences within the one tradition of witness to the God of Israel and his one plan of salvation. It is misleading, I believe, to speak of two peoples of God, or of two covenants, never mind to speak of two religions. While it was not specifically addressed to Jewish-Christian relations, this was the truth underscored also by the statement in 2000 by the Congregation for the Doctrine of the Faith, *Dominus Iesus.* It is not Christian imperialism but fidelity to revealed truth that requires Christians to say that Christ is Lord of all or he is not Lord at all. From the Jewish side, when after the Council the Catholic Church was formalizing its conversations with non-Christians, the Jewish interlocutors insisted that they not be grouped with the Vatican dicastery designed to deal with other religions but be included in conjunction with the secretariat for promoting Christian unity. There were political reasons for that insistence, not least having to do with the politics of the Middle East, but that arrangement has, I believe, much more profound implications than were perhaps realized at the time.

. . .

The salvation that is from the Jews cannot be proclaimed or lived apart from the Jews. This is not to say that innumerable Christians, indeed the vast majority of Christians, have not and do not live their Christian faith without consciousness of or contact with Jews. Obviously, they have and they do. The percentage of Christians involved in any form of Jewish-Christian dialogue is minuscule. Not much larger, it may be noted, is the percentage of Jews involved. In addition, significant dialogue is, for the most part, a North American phenomenon. It is one of the many things to which the familiar phrase applies, "Only in America." In Europe, for tragically obvious reasons, there are not enough Jews; in Israel, for reasons of growing tragedy, there are not enough Christians. Only in America are there enough Jews and Christians in a relationship of mutual security to make possible a dialogue that is unprecedented in two thousand years of history. The significance of this dialogue is in no way limited to America. The significance is universal. There is one people of Israel, as there is one Church. Providential purpose in history is a troubled subject, and the idea of America's providential purpose is even more troubled, but I suggest that we would not be wrong to believe that this dialogue, so closely linked to the American experience, is an essential part of the unfolding of the story of the world. Isaiah 43:19: "Behold, I am doing a new thing; now it springs forth, do you not perceive it?"

I think it fair to say that neither Christians nor Jews would have seen this new thing or have acted upon it were it not for the unspeakable tragedy of the Holocaust. This is recognized in *Dabru Emet*, which says of the Christian understanding of Judaism, "In the decades since the Holocaust, Christianity has changed dramatically." It should also be recognized that Judaism has, at least in large part, changed dramatically, as is evident in, for example, a statement such as *Dabru Emet*. Following World War II and accelerated by strident attacks on Christianity, and on Catholicism in particular, by such as Rolf Hochhuth and his 1963 play *The Deputy*, Jewish-Christian "dialogue" was for some years conducted mainly in the accusative mode. In this mode, the chief duty of Christians was to engage in rites of self-denigration for wrongs committed against Jews and Judaism. Some Jewish organizations and a good many self-depreciating Christians are still trapped in that mode. And it cannot be denied that, without the Jewish prosecution and subsequent Christian defensiveness, the self-examination resulting in the changes alluded to by *Dabru Emet* might not have happened. It is true that God writes straight with crooked lines.

Those Jews for whom "Never Again" means never enough of Christian self-denigration will continue to be with us, and we must try to contain our impatience, recognizing the burden of historical grievances and suspicions, and the institutional interest of some organizations in exploiting such grievances and suspicions. But in recent years the dialogue is becoming more truly a dialogue, as both Christians and Jews are at last catching up with, for instance, the proposal of David Novak in his important 1989 book, *Jewish-Christian Dia-*

logue. Indeed it may be said that, through the convoluted ways of history, we are at last catching up with the 1920s dialogue between Rosenzweig and Eugen Rosenstock, which was emphatically a dialogue about salvation—the salvation that comes from the Jews.

Still today there are Jews who resist a dialogue about salvation because that is necessarily a theological dialogue, and they do not want Christians to make Judaism a part of the Christian story. Similarly, there may be Christians who resent efforts such as *Dabru Emet* that tend to make Christianity part of the Jewish story. Advancing the dialogue requires, I believe, our recognition that the Christian story and the Jewish story are of theological interest only as they participate in the story of the one God of Israel. Along the way there are many stories, but ultimately the story of salvation, like the phrase "the people of God," has no plural.

Today it is commonly said that Christianity needs to reappropriate its Jewish dimensions, including the Jewishness of Jesus, and that is undoubtedly part of the truth. But this should not be understood as a matter of taking some parts from the Jewish house next door in order to rehabilitate our Christian house. We live in the same house, of which Christians say with St. Paul that the Jewish Christ is the cornerstone (Ephesians 2:20). To change the metaphor somewhat, we live in the house of the one people of God only as we live with the Jews of whom Jesus was—and eternally is—one. The second Person of the Holy

Trinity, true God and true man, is Jewish flesh. As is the eucharistic body we receive, as is the Body of Christ into which we are incorporated by Baptism. It is said that when John XXIII, then papal nuncio in Paris, first saw the pictures of the Jewish corpses at Auschwitz, he exclaimed, "There is the Body of Christ!"

All such insights are but variations on the words of Paul that must, for Christians, be ever at the center of our reflection on the mystery of living Judaism: "But if some of the branches were broken off and you, a wild olive shoot, were grafted in their place to share the richness of the olive tree, do not boast over the branches. If you do boast, remember it is not you that support the root, but the root that supports you. . . . So do not be proud, but stand in awe" (Romans 12:17ff). "Salvation is from the Jews." This people is not, as the aforementioned Bible commentator suggests, a "point of departure" but remains until the end of time our point of arrival. By the appointment of the God whom we worship, we travel together, joined in awe of one another, sometimes in fear of one another, always in argument with one another, until that final point of arrival when we shall know even as we are known (1 Corinthians 13:12).

When we Christians do not walk together with Jews, we are in danger of regressing to the paganism from which we emerged. Rosenzweig saw that gnosticism, pantheism, and assimilation to the idolatry of culture and nation are constant temptations for Christians. In 1929 he was prescient in foreseeing what would happen in Germany:

The nations have been in a state of inner conflict ever since Christianity with its supernational power came upon them. Ever since then, and everywhere, a Siegfried is at strife with that stranger, the man of the cross (*des gekreuzigten Mannes*), in his very appearance so suspect a character. . . . This stranger who resists the continued attempts to assimilate him to that nation's own self-idealization.

Marcionism was not a one-time heresy. New Marcions are ever at hand to seduce Christianity into becoming a culture-religion, a practical morality, or but another spirituality of self-fulfillment. Christianity does indeed seek to engage culture, provide a guide for living, and propose the way to human flourishing, but, reduced to any of these undoubtedly good ends, it is not Christianity. Liberal Protestant theology beginning in the nineteenth century was much preoccupied with the question of "the essence of Christianity," and, not incidentally, was contemptuous of Jews and Judaism. Christianity is not defined by an essence but by the man of the cross, a permanently suspect character, forever a stranger of that strange people, the Jews. Through Jesus the Jew, we Christians are anchored in history, defined not by an abstract essence but by a most particular story.

With respect to Judaism, Christians today are exhorted to reject every form of supersessionism, and so we should. To supersede means to nullify, to void, to make obsolete, to displace. The end of supersessionism, however, cannot and must not mean the end of the argument between Christians and Jews. We cannot settle into the comfortable interreligious politesse of mutual respect for positions deemed to be equally true. Christ and his Church do not supersede Judaism but they do continue and fulfill the story of which we are both part. Or so Christians must contend. It is the story that begins with Abraham who in the eucharistic canon we call "our father in faith."

There is no avoiding the much vexed question of whether this means that Jews should enter into the further fulfillment of the salvation story by becoming Christians. Christians cannot, out of a desire to be polite, answer that question in the negative. We can and must say that the ultimate duty of each person is to form his conscience in truth and act upon that discernment; we can and must say that there are great goods to be sought in dialogue apart from conversion; we can and must say that we reject proselytizing, which is best defined as evangelizing in a way that demeans the other; we can and must say that Jews and Christians need one another in many public tasks imposed upon us by a culture that is, in large part, in manifest rebellion against the God of Israel; we can and must say that there are theological, philosophical, and moral questions to be explored together, despite our differences regarding Messianic promise; we can and must say that friendship between Jew and Christian can be secured in shared love for the God of Israel; we can and must say that the historical forms we call Judaism and Christianity will be transcended, but not superseded, by the fulfillment of eschatological promise. But along the way to that final fulfillment we are locked in argument. It is an argument by which—for both Jew and Christian—conscience is formed, witness is honed, and friendship is deepened. This is our destiny, and this is our duty, as members of the one people of God—a people of God for which there is no plural.

We can do no better than Paul, who, at the end of his anguished ponderings in Romans 9 through 11, having arrived at the farthest reaches of analysis and explanation, dissolves into doxology:

O the depth of the riches and wisdom and knowledge of God! How unsearchable are His judgments and how inscrutable His ways! . . . For from Him and through Him and to Him are all things. To Him be glory forever. Amen.

Along the way to the eschatological resolution of our disagreements, Jews and Christians encourage one another to wait faithfully upon the Lord. Not all Jews and not all Christians agree with this way of understanding the matter. For instance, Christopher Leighton writes, "Plurality and difference are the inescapable realities of our existence, and any theological attempt to dissolve our diversity through appeals to a higher truth or a totalizing unity are suspect, even when projected against an eschatological horizon." He goes on to say that "the challenge for Christian theology is to accept, perhaps even celebrate, the gaps, the silences, the distances between us Christians and Jews." That is in some respects an attractive view and should not be dismissed as being no more than interreligious politesse. But it is, I believe, finally inadequate. "Totalizing" is, of course, a pejorative term, but it is precisely a definitive and comprehensive eschatological resolution that we await. Leighton is surely right to say, however, that along the way we should engage the Jewish people "as a mystery in whose company we may discover our own limits and in whose midst we may also discern new and unsuspected insights into ourselves, the world, and God."

It is precisely that spirit of discovery and discernment that marks the Second Vatican Council's "Declaration on the Relationship of the Church to Non-Christian Religions" (*Nostra Aetate*). Note that the declaration is about the Church, not simply about individual or group relations. Here the mystery of the Church encounters the mystery of the Jewish people. "As this sacred Synod searches into the mystery of the Church, it recalls the spiritual bond linking the people of the New Covenant with Abraham's stock." The Church does not go outside herself but more deeply within herself to engage Jews and Judaism. This is consonant with Rosenzweig's observation that Christianity becomes something else when it is not centered in the Jewish "man of the cross." *Nostra Aetate* continues: "Nor can [the Church] forget that she draws sustenance from the root of that good olive tree onto which have been grafted the wild olive branches of the Gentiles. Indeed, the Church believes that by his cross Christ, our Peace, reconciled Jew and Gentile, making them both one in himself (cf. Ephesians 2:14–16)." Note that the statement that the Church draws sustenance from the Jewish people is in the present tense. It is not simply that she drew sustenance in her beginnings; she now, and perhaps until the end of time, draws sustenance. Also with Muslims and others, *Nostra Aetate* enjoins understanding, respect, study, and dialogue, but only with reference to the Jews does the declaration say that we are dealing with the very mystery of the Church, and therefore the story of salvation.

At least for Catholics, *Nostra Aetate* marks the beginning of the present Jewish-Christian dialogue. That dialogue has produced many additional documents, official and unofficial, over the years. One may ask whether and, if so, how there have been advances over *Nostra Aetate* in Catholic understanding. That question necessarily engages the thought of John Paul II, who, it is universally acknowledged, has made unprecedented contributions to Catholic-Jewish relations. The extended reflection on Jews and Judaism in the Pope's remarkable little book *Crossing the Threshold of Hope* observes that "the New Covenant has its roots in the Old. The time when the people of the Old Covenant will be able to see themselves as part of the New is, naturally, a question to be left to the Holy Spirit." A purpose of the dialogue, if not *the* purpose of the dialogue, he adds, is "not to put obstacles in the way" of Jews coming to that recognition.

Note that he speaks of when, not whether, this will happen. As though to leave no doubt on this point, he goes on to discuss "how the New Covenant serves to fulfill all that is rooted in the vocation of Abraham, in God's covenant with Israel at Sinai, and in the whole rich heritage of the inspired Prophets who, hundreds of years before that fulfillment, pointed in the Sacred Scriptures to the One whom God would send in the 'fullness of time' (cf. Galatians 4:4)." Meanwhile, John Paul notes, the Church is carrying out the mission of Israel to the nations. He quotes approvingly a Jewish leader who said at a meeting, "I want to thank the Pope for all that the Catholic Church has done over the last two thousand years to make the true God known." We may recall in this connection that the Council's great Constitution on the Church, authoritatively setting forth her ecclesiological self-understanding, is titled *Lumen Gentium*, referring to the fulfillment of the vocation of Israel to be a light to the nations.

A useful reference for understanding the state of authoritative Catholic teaching is, of course, the *Catechism of the Catholic Church*. The Catechism has relatively little to say about Jews and Judaism in the post-biblical period, although, it must be admitted, the subject receives more attention than it probably does in the everyday piety, preaching, and catechesis of the Church. We read that "the people descended from Abraham would be the trustees of the promise made to the patriarchs, the chosen people, called to prepare for that day when God would gather all His children into the unity of the Church" (#60). That hint of supersessionism is immediately tempered by reference to the branches being grafted onto the root of Israel. At another point the Jewish character of the early Church is underscored, citing the statement of James in Acts, "How many thousands there are among the Jews of those who have believed, and they are all zealous for the Law" (#595). The discussion of the Second Coming refers to Romans 11 and "the 'full inclusion' of the Jews in the Messiah's salvation" (#674). The Catechism's fullest statement is found under the title "The Church and non-Christians," and deserves quotation in full:

> And when one considers the future, God's People of the Old Covenant and the new People of God tend towards similar goals: expectation of the coming (or the return) of the Messiah. But one awaits the return of the Messiah who died and rose from the dead and is recognized as Lord and Son of God, the other awaits the coming of a Messiah, whose features remain hidden till the end of time, and the latter waiting is accompanied by the drama of not knowing or of misunderstanding Christ Jesus. (#840)

While the Catechism is of course an authoritative presentation of magisterial teaching, one misses *Nostra Aetate*'s sense of the present-tense relationship to the Jewish people from which the Church learns and draws sustenance. Nor, in this connection, does the Catechism's treatment of eschatological expectation suggest a promised understanding or resolution of differences beyond that which the Church already knows and embodies.

One may usefully contrast David Novak's concluding thoughts on "the final redemption" in his book *Jewish-Christian Dialogue:*

> Until that time, we are all travelers passing through a vale of tears until we appear before God in Zion. Jews and Christians begin at the same starting point, and both are convinced that we will meet at the all-mysterious end. Yet we cannot deny that our appointed tasks in this world are very different and must remain so because the covenant is not the same for both of us. It is God alone who will bring us to our unknown destination in a time pleasing to Him. . . . Our dialogue might be able to show the world that the hope it needs for its very survival can only be the hope for its final redemption. . . . From creation and revelation comes our faith that God has not and will not abandon us or the world, that the promised redemption is surely yet to come.

Christians believe that the redemption that is surely yet to come has appeared in the Redeemer, Jesus the Christ—

although, to be sure, the appearance of the Kingdom, and therefore of the Messianic King in the fullness of glory, is not yet complete. Christians speak of the first advent and the second advent of the Christ, but there is another sense in which we may speak of his advent in the singular. And, if we think of his advent in the singular, we are still awaiting the final act. In the End Time, however, the Messiah will not appear as a stranger. Along the way, we have known his name and named his name. Yet Novak's sense of heightened expectation of something new—as distinct from the confirmation of a completely foregone and foreknown conclusion—seems to me the appropriate mode of eschatological hope also for Christians. Knowing that we do not yet know even as we are known, we know that there is more to be known. Dialogue between Jews and Christians should be marked by an element of curiosity, by shared exploration of what we do not know, and perhaps cannot know until the End Time.

For this reason, too, I believe our passage from John 4—"Salvation is from the Jews"—should have a more prominent place in the dialogue than has been the case. The passage nicely combines the "now" and "not yet" of life lived eschatologically. The "now" is unequivocal. The woman said to him, "I know that Messiah is coming and when he comes he will show us all things." Jesus answers, "I who speak to you am he." The "now" and "not yet" are then exquisitely joined in the words of Jesus: "The hour is coming when neither on this mountain nor in Jerusalem will you worship the Father. . . . The hour is coming, and now is, when the true worshipers will worship the Father in spirit and truth, for such the Father seeks to worship Him."

Here one can agree with Bultmann in recognizing in these words an intimation of the vision of Revelation 21:22–26: "And I saw no temple in the city, for its temple is the Lord God the Almighty and the Lamb. And the city has no need of sun or moon to shine upon it, for the glory of God is its light, and its lamp is the Lamb. By its light shall the nations walk; and the kings of the earth shall bring their glory into it, and its gates shall never shut by day—and there shall be no night; they shall bring into it the glory and the honor of the nations." That is the mission of Israel fulfilled as *lumen gentium.*

Along the way to that fulfillment, Christians and Jews will disagree about whether we can name the name of the Lamb. And when it turns out that we Christians have rightly named the Lamb ahead of time, there will be, as St. Paul reminds us, no reason for boasting; for in the beginning, all along the way, and in the final consummation, it will be evident to all that the Lamb—which is to say salvation—is from the Jews. There will be no boasting for many reasons, not least because boasting is unseemly and there will be nothing unseemly in the Kingdom of God. But chiefly there will be no boasting because then all glory will be to the God of Abraham, Isaac,

Jacob, and Jesus for His inclusion of us, all undeserving, in the story of salvation. Salvation is from the Jews, then, not as a "point of departure" but as the continuing presence and promise of a point of arrival—a point of arrival that we, Christians and Jews, together pray that we will together reach.

GABRIEL SAID REYNOLDS

THE OTHER ISLAM

Whether from hardliners who warn of a "conflict of civilizations" or from academic apologists who insist that Islam is "a religion of peace," we are often given impressions of Islam that exaggerate the uniformity of the world's more than one billion Muslims and underplay their diversity. My friend Mojtaba is a symbol of this diversity.

Mojtaba hails from the holiest city in Iran: Qomm, site of the holy shrine dedicated to Fâtima, the daughter of Muhammad and wife of Ali, the first Imâm. Mojtaba fondly remembers the waves of pilgrims who would come to visit the shrine each year, Shi'ite Muslims from all over the world. (Roughly 16 percent of Muslims are Shi'ites; the vast majority of Muslims are Sunni, while others belong to smaller sects.) Qomm is also home to the most important schools of religious training for mullahs (Shi'ite clerics). The Ayatollah Khomeini studied there himself until 1963, when he was forced into exile in Turkey. Mojtaba's father was likewise trained as a mullah in Qomm, during which time he became friends with Khomeini.

The two stayed in touch after Khomeini's exile. Some years later, when Khomeini had moved to the second holy Shi'ite city of Najaf, in Iraq, Mojtaba's father also went to Najaf as a religious teacher and brought his family with him. Mojtaba fondly recalls meeting Khomeini there as a child. Mojtaba was also there when, on March 1, 1978, Khomeini returned triumphantly to Qomm in the wake of the Revolution. Until the death of Khomeini, Mojtaba's father was one of his close friends and religious advisors.

Although I never asked him directly, I came to understand that it was due to this influence that Mojtaba got a position with the Islamic government of Iran. A few years later, he was appointed to work at the Iranian cultural institute in Beirut, where I went to study Persian. I remember distinctly my first meeting with Mojtaba, who wears a traditional beard but Western dress. Emerging from an old wooden elevator that had put my life in jeopardy, I entered a nondescript classroom to find a short, balding Lebanese man and Mojtaba, who smiled and greeted me with the traditional Muslim salutation, *"as-Salâmu 'alaykum!"* I had prepared myself to meet very traditional Shi'ites at the institute, and the vision of Mojtaba before me was just what I expected. Yet looks can be deceiving.

Make no mistake: Mojtaba is a devout Muslim, and proudly so. He brings his son, Mahdi, to the mosque each Friday and he fasts during Ramadan. His wife, Ashraf Sadat, wears a headscarf (although it surprised me to see how she wears it—pulled back a bit, so that the front of her hair is showing). And Mojtaba met his wife in the most traditional fashion. His mother sent out word in Qomm that her son had a good job and was ready to marry. Mom then visited a number of families to see the daughters and speak with the parents. Eventually she came up with a short list, and Mojtaba, when he returned home to Qomm, prepared to go out and see the candidates for himself. At the very first house, he met Ashraf Sadat, an energetic, fair-skinned woman with a wide smile and sharp eyes that immediately win your attention. After a half-hour meeting, Mojtaba was satisfied. So was Ashraf Sadat, and they were married. The marriage ceremony consists of nothing more than a meeting between the husband, his father, the bride's father, and the shaykh. It is more a legal than a spiritual ceremony: a bride-gift is offered and a contract is drawn up that sets certain stipulations regarding divorce and inheritance, among other matters.

This is exactly the type of background that I expected from the son of a mullah and an officer of the Islamic republic of Iran. What I did not expect was the feelings that Mojtaba would express to me privately about religion. One day we sat together through a Christian/Muslim dialogue in Beirut where the topic of the day was "Heaven, Hell, and the End of the World." Both the Christians and the Muslims at the meeting were boasting about their rival visions of the afterlife, imagined in some detail.

After the meeting Mojtaba and I were walking silently up a steep street, as old Mercedes taxis roared by us. At a certain point he stopped, looked at me, and said in his soft voice, "You know, Gabriel, all of this talk about heaven is really stupid. It is like they are arguing about what the peak of a cloud-covered mountain looks like. Nobody in that room has been to the top of that mountain."

Another time I was bold enough to complain to Mojtaba about the situation of non-Muslims in Iran. In particular, that year there were a number of Iranian Jews who had been arrested and charged with spying for Israel. I told him that many Jews in America were upset about these events. More generally, I said, Jews are nervous in general about anti-Semitism in the Islamic world. Many think that Muslims are by nature anti-Jewish because of the way that Jews were eliminated in Muhammad's Medina. This was one of the few times that I saw the mild-mannered Mojtaba get angry. He raised his voice over mine to declare that the stories of Muhammad eliminating the Jews were falsifications. "It's impossible!" he said. "Muhammad was a gentle prophet. His enemies made this up about him!"

Now the more radical shaykh, Ziad, with whom I studied in Beirut, also believed in conspiracies, but they tended to be stories of how Jews and Americans had a worldwide alliance to undermine and destroy Islam. In Mojtaba's case, the conspiracies involved radical Muslims like Ziad, who tried to turn Muhammad into a reflection of their own violent selves. This was a small revelation about the ongoing struggle *within* Islam over what exactly the prophet and his religion will look like.

The Mystical Colors of Shi'ite Islam

Yet the difference between Mojtaba and Ziad is much more profound than the question of Muhammad's character. If Ziad sees the world as a big competition, Muslim vs. non-Muslim, Mojtaba has no interest playing that game. Instead, Mojtaba sees *all* of the religious life in mystical colors, and he would often interrupt me to share a line of Persian poetry that expressed my thoughts in a much simpler, and much more profound fashion. To Mojtaba, and many Iranians like him, the poets Rumi and Hafez are sources of religious knowledge almost equal to that of the Qur'an. Like Fâtima's shrine in Qomm, the tomb of Hafez in the southern Iranian city of Shiraz attracts crowds of pilgrims every year. And the poetry of Hafez and Rumi is hardly what you would expect, with its tributes to wine and other seemingly un-Islamic themes. I was quite surprised one day when Mojtaba jumped up from his seat in the middle of our Persian lesson to illustrate a point on the board. He wrote out a line of Rumi's poetry, from heart, which compared prayer to looking into the large brown eyes of a beautiful girl.

On another occasion Mojtaba and I were sitting in on a Christian/Muslim dialogue session when a shaykh quoted a verse from the Qur'an where the children of Abraham are asked by God to whom they belong: *a-lastu bi-rabbikum?* "Am I not your Lord?" (Qur'an 7:172). To many Muslims this verse expresses a fundamental religious lesson, that God is *al-qadîr*, the All-powerful, and we are in His control. Hence Qur'an

5:118: "If you punish them, well they are your servants. If you forgive them, well you are the Mighty, the Wise." To Mojtaba, however, the mention of *a-lastu bi-rabbikum* brought up an entirely different set of associations. He grabbed my notebook and wrote down a piece of Hafez's poetry, which began with the words *ruz-e a-lastu*. *Ruz-e* is Persian for "the day of" and *a-lastu* is the Qur'anic Arabic from the first passage above for "am I not?" The phrase "the day of 'am I not'" refers to the covenant that took place between God and man before the world was created. At that moment, God collectively confronted all the future souls with the question that would determine their individual destiny: "Am I not your Lord?"

Yet on another level, Hafez's phrase expresses something very present. To Hafez (and Mojtaba), *ruz-e a-lastu* is the timeless moment when believers encounter the face of God in their spiritual journey. Then they, too, are mystically present at the day of the covenant, and confronted with the same decision. We all are confronted with the same decision.

The Space Between God and Man

This focus on the individual's religious journey, on a personal connection with the divine, is an essential element of Shi'ite Islam. Much effort has been expended in Sunni Islam to separate God from His creation, in order to preserve His perfect oneness. This is the basis of the Qur'anic critique of the Christian doctrine of the incarnation: "For God is one god! Far be it from Him to have an offspring! All of the heavens and the earth are His!" (4:171). "Say: He is one God, the eternal God. He does not beget and He is not begotten and He does not have any peer" (112). According to much of Sunni Islam, and in particular the reformist Islam which is on the rise today, the perfect oneness and transcendence of God means that there can be no intermediaries between creator and creature. Thus, the Wahhâbis, adherents of a Sunni reformist movement that is the dominant form of Islam in Saudi Arabia, have meticulously destroyed the tombs of saints that used to be the center of pilgrimages there. The Wahhâbis maintain that such devotion is a form of idolatry, as God alone should be the center of worship. In Iran, by contrast, there are no such prohibitions. On the contrary, religious leaders (and merchants) strongly encourage pilgrimages to saints' tombs.

Idolatry is a serious matter for all Muslims, of course, as it is for Christians. Yet the question of what idolatry consists of is interpreted much more rigorously in Sunni Islam. This can be seen not only in the question of saints' tombs but also in Islamic art. From early on there was a prohibition against figural representation in the Islamic world; that is, neither God nor angels nor humans were represented in paintings or sculpture. This iconoclasm, present also in Jewish tradition and in different periods of Christian tradition, was intended to ensure that mere paintings or sculptures did not themselves become the object of worship. Thus, Islamic art collections, even at American museums, will often consist of only pottery and cal-

ligraphy. Sunni Muslims have, until the modern era, followed
this ban quite closely. Even in recent times we have witnessed
the Taliban of Afghanistan prohibit all photos, including both
television and drawings in medical textbooks, out of a fear of
idolatry. But among Shi'ite Muslims the ban on figural representation has often been rejected or reinterpreted. Hence the
remarkable tradition of Iranian miniature paintings.

In Reformist Sunni Islam there is a great empty space
between God, the Lord (*al-rabb*), and man, the servant (*al-
'abd*)—a space that should not be filled up by men or images
of men. Even the position of Muhammad, the final bearer of
the Islamic message to mankind, described in the Qur'an as a
"mercy for those who believe" (9:61), is sharply defined so as
to avoid any blurring of the divine unity. Yet in Shi'ite Islam,
the distance between God and man is filled with hosts of
intercessors. Shi'ite theologians speak about the necessity of
having an Imâm, a divinely appointed religious leader, always
present on earth. He is called the "proof" (*hujja*) of God, and
without him it is imagined that the world would quite literally
fall apart.

The first of these Imâms, as mentioned above, was Ali, the
cousin and son-in-law of Muhammad. In Shi'ism there is an
especial privilege accorded to the blood relations and descen-
dents of Muhammad. Shi'ites maintain that God not only
chose Muhammad as his prophet but also his entire family to
be special custodians of the prophetic message. Thus, it was a
particularly evil day when Ali was deprived of his rightful

position by the Sunni leaders 'Umar and Abû Bakr, the latter of whom became the first caliph of the Sunnis. Ali himself finally became caliph, after having been passed over twice more, but his brief reign was marked by rebellion and civil war. In 661, Ali was murdered by a treacherous group among his own followers, and the position of Imâm passed on to his two sons by Fâtima, Muhammad's daughter: first Hasan and then Husayn. Shi'ites record how Muhammad demanded that his community be loyal to his grandchildren. A Shi'ite tradition maintains that one day while Muhammad was holding his two young grandchildren on his lap, he looked at the people around and declared: "Whoever loves me, loves them. Whoever hates me, hates them."

Fâtima is referred to by Shi'ites as *al-Zahrâ'*, "The Resplendent One," and with her husband, Ali, and their children she intercedes in heaven for the Shi'ite community on earth. This image is in many ways an excellent point for Christians to begin dialogue with Shi'ites. For the picture of Ali and Fâtima at the heavenly throne is not entirely different from that of Jesus and Mary interceding with God the father on behalf of the world. Some more extreme Shi'ite groups, such as the Alawites of Syria (the sect to which Bashar al-Asad, the Syrian president, belongs), even consider Ali to be divine. Muhammad, according to them, was merely the mouthpiece of the more important figure, Ali, just as Aaron was a mouthpiece for Moses.

Martyrdom

The parallels between Shi'ite Islam and Christianity (especially Catholic and Orthodox Christianity) can be drawn even further. If the axis of Christian history and spirituality is the martrydom of Christ, then that of Shi'ite Islam is the martyrdom of Husayn. His older brother Hasan, who became Imâm after his father, died in the year 670. Some Shi'ite sources maintain that he was poisoned by one of his many wives, who was paid off for the job by a Sunni. In fact, it is a common Shi'ite belief that each of the first eleven Imâms was martyred by the Sunnis. While this is more an article of faith than of history, it expresses a deeper truth about the historical experience of the Shi'ites. For while the history books of Sunnis are filled with the stories of great conquering generals, who defeated and killed their enemies, the history books of Shi'ites (like those of Christians) are filled with the stories of tragic heroes, who were defeated and killed by their enemies.

The most celebrated of these heroes is Husayn, who became Imâm after his brother. In 680 Husayn and his small band of loyal followers were met by a much larger Sunni force in the plains outside of the Iraqi city of Kerbala. The Sunnis, so the Shi'ite accounts tell us, engaged Husayn and his forces in battle. Husayn and his small band fought valiantly, but were overcome and brutally massacred. As on the Friday when Jesus was led to Golgotha, evil reigned. At Husayn's death, the sun became dark and the skies rained blood. Husayn's decapitated head chanted a final verse from the Qur'an. This scene is a microcosm of the entire Shi'ite experience as understood from within: a small, oppressed, and innocent group fighting righteously for "true" Islam and accepting martyrdom. It is ritually replayed every year in Shi'ite communities throughout the world in a type of passion play (not altogether different from the Stations of the Cross) known as *ta'ziya*. Processions also associated with the event are often filled with young men who beat or flagellate themselves, so as to participate in the sufferings of Husayn. Indeed, it is believed by Shi'ites that the sufferings which Husayn endured bring forgiveness upon his community for their sins. Husayn is their suffering savior.

And yet connections with the passion of Jesus or with the martyrdom of the early Christians should not be exaggerated. For the concept of martyrdom is quite different in the two traditions. Husayn, after all, died with a sword in his hand, not "like a lamb that is led to the slaughter." The Islamic martyr is a battlefield martyr, and from this perspective is totally unlike the early Christian martyrs who died peacefully, like Stephen, Peter, Polycarp, Lucy, and Agatha.

The key point here, to which Christians *can* relate, is the personal connection that Shi'ites like Mojtaba find with Husayn, as they do with his father, Ali, and mother, Fâtima. In Shi'ism, individual believers develop personal relationships with these figures, characterized by love and emulation. At a Shi'ite bookshop outside the headquarters of Hizballah, a young man gave me a booklet filled with sayings on the praise of Fâtima.

On the cover was a light blue veil (with no face portrayed) and glowing by the light of white candles. The effect was not unlike portrayals of the Virgin Mary in pamphlets that I have seen from Lourdes, France, and Syracuse, Italy.

The Hidden Imâm

There is another character who is critical in the Shi'ite drama: the final and hidden Imâm. The line of Imâms continued through Ali, Hasan, and Husayn, and so on until the year 874, when the eleventh Imâm, al-Hasan al-'Askarî, was murdered at the hands of the Sunnis. As far as the Sunnis knew, 'Askarî had no male offspring, and so they had wiped out the line of Shi'ite Imâms forever. Yet Shi'ites claim that 'Askarî did indeed have a son, who was born under miraculous circumstances, an infant whom few had seen, since he was kept carefully concealed from the Sunnis. A midwife who witnessed the scene gives the following account of the birth of the twelfth and final Imâm:

> I woke up with the sense of my Master, so I lifted up her [the Imâm's mother] covering and he (peace be upon him) was prostrating. . . . I held him (peace be upon him) close to me and he was entirely clean. . . . [al-Hasan al-'Askarî] said to him, "Speak, my son!" And he said, "I bear witness that there is no god but God alone—He has no partner— and that Muhammad is the messenger of God." Then he

blessed the Commander of the Faithful [Ali], and all of the
Imâms until he stopped with his father.

The Imâm's miraculous ability of speech as a child is a clear
parallel to the Qur'anic story of Jesus' miraculous speech in the
cradle (Qur'an 3:46, 19:29–30). This is not the only parallel
between the final Imâm and Jesus. Like the Jesus of the Islamic
tradition, the Imâm did not die a natural death; rather, he was
taken by God into a state of occultation. But while God
brought Jesus directly up into heaven (see Qur'an 4:158), He
preserved the final Imâm on earth, keeping him hidden from
the rest of humanity. Occasionally we hear accounts of Shi'ites
who claim to have actually seen or spoken to the Imâm, usually on the Hajj in Mecca, which he is said to perform every
year. And because the world would end without the presence
of the Imâm on earth (even if he is hidden), he must remain
here until the end of the world.

When that time comes, Jesus and the Hidden Imâm will
emerge together, inflicting bloody revenge against the enemies of the Shi'ites and establishing a reign of perfect Islamic
justice in advance of the last judgment. They will form an
apocalyptic tag team, slaughtering the Sunnis, defeating the
Antichrist, breaking crosses of churches, and killing all of the
swine. These last two acts are clearly symbolic of the ultimate
victory of Islam over Christianity. They reflect the fact that
these apocalyptic traditions were not composed at the time of
Muhammad (as Islamic tradition maintains), but rather several

centuries later, when the Islamic Empire was embroiled in a fierce struggle with the Christian Byzantine Empire. Their effect, however, is to help preserve for Muslims today the idea that Islam and Christianity are locked in an undying religious warfare, that Christianity is destined to be Islam's arch-rival until the last judgment. Hence the obsession with the Crusades that marks fundamentalist Islamic rhetoric.

The Hidden Imâm is also referred to as *al-Qâ'im bi-'l-sayf,* "the one who rises with the sword," describing the manner in which he will return to establish justice upon the earth. His return is not unlike the picture in the Book of Revelation, where Jesus is described as a heavenly warrior: "In his right hand he held seven stars, and from his mouth came a sharp, two-edged sword, and his face was like the sun shining with full force" (Revelation 1:16). There is a popular expression in Christianity, that the first time the Lord came as a lamb, but he will return as a lion. The vengeance of the Lord upon evildoers has been, in a way, postponed: *vindicta mihi,* says the Lord ("vengeance is my job!" [Romans 12:19]). This postponement has allowed Christians in some traditions to take a nonviolent stance on political questions, since the judgment of wrongdoers will take place in the next life or at the end of the world, whichever comes first.

So it is with Shi'ism. The very fact that the Hidden Imâm is a fearsome, militant character allows Shi'ites to embrace political quietism, since the day for activism has not yet arrived. This stands out in stark contrast to the politically activist instincts of Sunni Islam. While Sunnis traditionally have worked to re-establish the Islamic Empire of Muhammad and his immediate followers, Shi'ites have prayed for the "coming out" *(khurûj)* of the Imâm to establish the Islamic Empire that never came into being, due to the treachery of the Sunnis. Thus, the mention of the Hidden Imâm's name is quickly followed by the phrase "May God speed his appearance." I remember watching a call-in telephone program on the Lebanese station al-Manâra, which is run by Hizballah, the Shi'ite militia funded by Iran and Syria. The program had all the trappings of an American talk show about teenage pregnancy or alien abductions, but the discussion was all focused on when and how the Hidden Imâm will arrive.

The Shi'ite approach to politics also makes me think of the attitude of certain ultra-Orthodox Jewish groups in Brooklyn who are vehemently opposed to the state of Israel. They maintain that a true Israel can only be founded by God acting through the Messiah, when he appears. This is a mentality of waiting and praying, of political quietism. It has a subversive effect upon the categories that distinguish the fundamentalist way of thinking. Thus, for Shi'ites, the world is not divided into the House of Islam *(dâr al-islâm)* and the House of War *(dâr al-harb)*, as Sunnis maintain. For inside the House of Islam is a smaller community, the Shi'ite community, which they call the House of Faith *(dâr al-imân)*. The primary duty of the Shi'ite, then, is not to confront the House of War in battle (although that is not necessarily ruled out) but to convert the House of Islam, through peaceful means, to Shi'ism.

Political Activism, Political Quietism

Having said all of this, it is not wholly accurate to depict Shi'ite Islam as non-political, a polar opposite to the political Islam of Sunnism. After all, it was the cataclysmic events of 1978 in Shi'ite Iran that brought political Islam to the center of the world's attention. For those theologians sympathetic to Khomeini's movement, the suffering of the Shi'ite Imâms at the hands of their enemies should not inspire quietism, but rather revolution. Khomeini's Islam was, after all, politically activist. Moreover, he urgently sought to unify both Sunni and Shi'ite Muslims against America (*shaytân-e bazorg*, "the Great Satan") and the Soviet Union. In a speech on September 12, 1980, Khomeini declared:

At a time when all the Muslims in the world are about to join together and achieve mutual understanding between the different schools of thought in Islam, in order to deliver their nations from the foul grasp of the superpowers; at a time when the arms of the Eastern and Western oppressors are about to be foreshortened in Iran, by means of unity of purpose and reliance on God Almighty—precisely at this time, the Great Satan has summoned its agents and instructed them to sow dissension among the Muslims by every imaginable means, giving rise to hostility and dispute among brothers in faith who share the belief in God's unity, so that nothing will stand in the way of complete domination and plunder.

There are other Shi'ite movements, too, that have a political and militaristic tone. Lebanon has witnessed political Shi'ite Islam in the Amal movement (particularly when it was led by Musa Sadr) and more recently in Hizballah, whose fiery young leader, Hasan Nasrallah, excites both Shi'ites and Sunnis to join the jihad against Israel and America.

Yet these Shi'ite activist movements find their ideological underpinning not in classical sources but rather in a concept developed largely by Khomeini himself: *wilayat-e faqih*, "rulership of the religious lawyer." By this phrase Khomeini intends that, until the return of the Hidden Imâm, it is the responsibility of the religious lawyers to rule and to establish a just Islamic state. It should be remembered that both Amal and Hizballah are not so much independent manifestations of activist Shi'ite Islam as much as satellites of Khomeini's movement and philosophy. Both groups are funded by Iran, without whose support that would be left out in the cold.

Moreover, the idea of *wilayat-e faqih* has by no means gone without opposition in the Shi'ite community. In fact, today it is no exaggeration to say that the Islamic government in Iran has lost the support of the Iranian people who, through underground newspapers, student marches, and even demonstrations after soccer games, are calling for a secular form of government. Meanwhile, the son of the former shah, Reza Pahlavi, is openly calling for the overthrow of the government and his own political ambitions are not hard to detect.

A Dinner with Two Shi'ite Seminarians

It is hard to avoid the conclusion that Shi'ism provides many more entry points for a dialogue with the West than does Sunnism. This is something that I also felt on a very personal level. During my studies with the radical Shaykh Ziad and my interactions with other Sunnis in Lebanon, I quickly became exhausted by the never-ending religious polemic. I remember a taxi ride that I suffered through, in a pouring winter rainstorm, all the way from Beirut to a small village outside Damascus. For four hours I listened to the cab driver tell me why Islam is the perfect religion, since it contains all of Judaism and Christianity and then adds more. The climax of his argument was that Islam permitted a man to divorce and remarry as often as he wants, whereas Christianity kept man in the prison of marriage. (At least he was honest.) When I recounted this story to a friend who had spent many years in North Africa and the Middle East, he chuckled and said that when it came to religious polemic, Syria was nothing compared to Egypt. He recounted a six-hour bus ride from Isma'iliyya to Cairo during which the fellow next to him, an enlisted soldier, recited the Qur'an at the top of his voice without cease. No one had the gall to ask him to recite quietly to himself, for fear of seeming anti-Islamic. So I entered into my studies with Shi'ite teachers in Lebanon expecting more of the same, a bit apprehensive of the headache-inducing polemic that I might encounter. Yet I found no polemic, no headaches.

I registered in a second Persian class with twelve other religious Shi'ites, several of whom were members of Hizballah. During the three months that we studied together, the most aggressive comment that I received was from a woman who was confused why some Lebanese Christians refuse to call themselves Arabs, declaring themselves instead to be Phoenicians. Knowing that I lived in a Christian neighborhood, she asked me to find out why. One day, when another student noticed that I was wearing a tie, he said, "You know the Ayatollah Khomeini delivered a ruling that men should not wear ties, since they are Western and not authentic Islamic dress."

Later I learned that some of the students, most likely the Hizballah members, were trying to find out from Mojtaba if I was a Jew, and one of them was convinced that I was a spy. Yet they never said anything to me about it, and these "accusations" were not so unusual anyway. By and large the students had the utmost respect for me as a Christian. In fact, I felt so comfortable that one day I took one of them aside and explained how exhausted I was from the religious polemic that

Shaykh Ziad was continually confronting me with. He looked at me kindly and said, "You should study with a Shi'ite. All of those Sunnis are fanatics."

The religious questions that absorbed many of my Shi'ite friends generally had nothing to do with proving Islam right and Christianity wrong, but rather focused on questions that were common to both traditions. One night I was invited to a dinner in the heavily Shi'ite southern suburbs of Beirut, the neighborhood where the American hostages were kept tied to a radiator during the war, the neighborhood where Lebanese army soldiers are no longer to be found but rather Hizballah militiamen in their place. I was invited there to meet a couple of young Shi'ite theology students from Africa, who were very curious to meet me. The two students, one from South Africa (whose father is an Afrikaans convert to Islam, while his mother is an Indian Muslim) and the other from Burkina Faso, welcomed me into to the spacious apartment. I took off my shoes, sat down on the brown carpet, and was promptly offered a cup of scalding Turkish coffee and a sweet red fig. I thanked them and looked at the two smiling students hesitantly, waiting for them to begin another discussion about why the Bible is corrupt and the doctrine of the Trinity is illogical. But Ahmed, the South African, surprised me with his first question: "So, do you consider that God or man is the creator of human actions?"

With that we entered into an age-old philosophical dispute that has haunted both the Islamic and Christian traditions.

This, happily enough, was a point where Catholic and Shi'ite traditions are agreed: man is the creator of his own actions and is judged by God for the actions that he creates. A Sunni, in contrast, would say that God is indeed the creator of those acts and that man, by "acquiring" those acts, is judged for them, even if that means acquiring an act that will lead one to eternal damnation. This would mean, for example, that God leads a believer into unbelief, and then punishes the poor sap in hell for that unbelief. Hence the famous saying, which is rejected by Shi'ites but accepted by Sunnis: "These to Heaven and I care not, and these to Hell and I care not." There is no question for a Sunni of calling God unjust for such an act, for He is above human conceptions of good and evil. Man has no right meddling with things that he simply cannot understand.

In contrast, Shi'ite theologians have tenaciously maintained throughout time that God is not only good and just but that He is good and just in a way that we can understand. God could not judge man by actions that He compelled man to commit and still be a just God. This is precisely the conclusion that Catholic theology (as represented by Thomas Aquinas, for example) has reached. Thus, the answer that I came up with was precisely what the Shi'ite theologians wanted to hear, and we were all quite pleased that we had arrived at a consensus on the question of predestination. Ahmed exclaimed, almost gleefully, "The Sunni view makes a laughingstock out of the Day of Judgment!" And I added, "So does the Calvinist view!"

Some scholars have concluded that the Shi'ite openness to such questions relates to the historical tragedies of the Shi'ite community. Since for the most part Shi'ites have not been able to establish their own regimes, and since the awaited Hidden Imâm has not yet appeared, they have developed the sciences of speculative theology and philosophy. Thus, it is sometimes said that Sunnis care simply about the acquisition of knowledge (*'ilm*), but Shi'ites care about the development of wisdom (*hikma*).

But this is to caricature the Sunni tradition, as I have been in danger of doing throughout. Nor do I want to leave readers with the impression that all Sunnis are fundamentalists and all Shi'ites moderate and progressive. In fact, the twentieth-century movement sometimes called Islamic modernism is primarily led by Sunnis. And I haven't even mentioned the vibrant Sufi tradition, which emphasizes ecstatic experience and personal intimacy with God and which has drawn many many Western converts to Islam. I do hope, however, that I have suggested something of the diversity within the Muslim world, and in particular the striking affinities that cry out for exploration in dialogue between Christians and Shi'ites.

LONGING

Not so much a thought as a pinpoint on the horizon of thought; not so much appearing as the world slowly rolling to reveal it; not so much the world but a breath of eternity, releasing this infinitesimal Yes. Between meetings and paperwork and meal plans and financial decisions and the seemingly more substantial everything of life, it drifts quietly toward resolution, takes hold in a little crevice of mind, and begins. There is time now in the cluttered shuffle of things for only this tiny Yes.

We have been speaking of it, my husband and I, with few and careful words, as it has a kind of sacred piquance. To speak of it aloud too much might flatten or dishonor it. But this slip of assent will grow.

For me, this Yes arises from within the kind of human hunger that memory forms and feeds. Five years after Miriam was born, three after Jacob, I remember their babyhoods with a mute, heart-clutching nostalgia. This is a fresh longing now for an experience (or the preserved portion of it) I have lived before: first, the deep attentiveness of pregnancy, then the harrowing intensity of birth, then that surrender of the self to demands that press the boundaries of endurance and to a small person who, once here, will make any previous life seem impossibly incomplete.

There are other strands of hunger tangled up in this, too, spindly little shabby ones: a weary desire to escape the routine, the inconvenient, the tedious difficulties of getting up, going to work, coming home. I half know I'm looking for change and variety, excitement, risk, for an escape.

But deeper than all that is the peculiar hunger of the body itself. Not for sexual union, although of course that human longing for intimacy is caught up, masterfully, with the desire to create. The body-hunger I feel is low in the gut, a kind of emptiness repeatedly reaching out to be filled. It is ancient, archetypal.

I came across a strangely unembroidered, uncontextualized oracle in the biblical book of Proverbs that tells me I'm not the only one to feel the womb itself seem to cry out in this hunger:

There are three things that are never satisfied,
four that never say, "Enough!":
the grave, the barren womb,
land, which is never satisfied with water,
and fire, which never says, "Enough!"

The longing to create life is elemental, on the level of fire, earth, and death. The steadily humming tissues and organs, as they play out their unconscious patterns, long to serve something spiritual, to touch the eternal. Perhaps the mortal body snatches out toward the immortal body. I believe that immortality is not a matter of disembodied spirits floating about in some cloudy afterlife, but of flesh, the carnal, renewed and perfected beyond our imaginings, reborn with all of creation. It does not seem strange to me, then, that our physical bodies lean hard, with our souls, toward the eternal.

Laughter

I've been taught since childhood that the Bible is an instructive place for exploring elementally human things, and no part of it is more elemental than the book of Genesis, with its ancient stories telling us like vivid and persistent dreams the deep truths of humanity, God, and ourselves. Womb-hunger, I find, is a deep current in the familiar stories of the matriarchs. Sarah, Rebekah, Rachel are all "barren" for a time until the Lord "remembers" or "listens to" their pleas. For Sarah and Abraham, barrenness is an especially wrenching and puzzling problem, as God promises early in their story to make Abraham the father of a great nation. But chapters go by and no conception occurs. Some commentators, particularly feminist ones, see the pattern of barrenness, delay, and joyful fulfillment in these stories as one important way in which ancient

Hebrew writers asserted the superior power of their one, true, and, not incidentally, masculine God over the fertility-goddess religions among which Hebrew monotheism arose. Fertility, these ancient writers wished to emphasize, comes not from goddess-idols or the earth's cycles, but from God alone. This erasure of the power of feminine divinity by a superior, masculine divine power follows the pattern of many Near Eastern civilizations, in fact. The matriarchal gives way to the patriarchal, and a world of woes for women ensues.

But the delay between desire and physical conception in the Genesis narratives is more than a compositional device in service of religious orthodoxy. It is a basic matter of human experience. Perhaps the barren times in these stories, and later, in a more detailed and poignant version in the story of Hannah, emphasize the power of God over the womb, but they also offer a pattern of longing to participate with the creator in the creation of something greater than oneself. Cultural historians might suggest that these women wanted children because a son was their only avenue to status and a remembered name. Barrenness, in their culture, would make them a shamed nothing, a cipher. But their longing, and that of their husbands, spreads outward into the symbolic, signifying all our longings to defy death. It is located not just in their own time and place, but in the human soul.

Moreover, in the songs of joy they sing when the babies finally do come, these ancient mothers recognize the power of God let loose within them. Rather than being silent vessels of the masculine God's power, they are given voices; they express longing and anger and frustration and then triumph when their longings are fulfilled. Biblical scholar Phyllis Trible shows that the God of these narratives is consistently described throughout the Hebrew scriptures as the God of compassion, and the Hebrew verb to express having compassion (*racham*) is directly related to the word for womb (*rechem*). The woman's womb is the physical metaphor for the abundant love of God. Thus the power of God over fertility remains a feminine power, and the experience of the mother in bringing forth life parallels the power of the Creator to bring forth all things. The words of the First Mother, Eve, on the birth of her first son echo this relationship of co-creation: "With the help of the Lord I have brought forth a man." (The name Cain is a pun on the Hebrew for "brought forth" or "gotten.") The "getting" of a new person is a source of joy and delight, just as the creation of the world is depicted as a source of delight to the Creator, a delight emphasized not only by the declarations of "very good," but also by the earthy word plays of the Hebrew account. Sarah's response to her son Isaac's birth best expresses this joy. When Isaac is finally born in her old age, she acknowledges both her earlier disbelief at this possibility as well as her joy at the reality of it by naming her son "he laughs"—a cleverly honest name—and she remarks: "God has brought me laughter, and everyone who hears about this will laugh with me." God has done this, and it is marvelous in her weary, shining eyes.

This is the laughter Ron and I hunger and wait for now, the laughter of participating in creation, of letting our flawed, sometimes doubtful, foolish, cynical, selfish, but ultimately loved and glorious selves experience in our bodies the delight and power of God.

Awakening

I had experienced the hunger and its fulfillment twice before, and it lay dormant for a time. But it was reawakened the spring my daughter was four, my son was two, and I thought I had become pregnant without planning to. It began with queer feelings in the stomach and tingling in the breasts. Long before my period was due, I started obsessing: *What if . . . ?* I was rather alarmed; this was no time for a new baby. My job was far too demanding and I was too unsettled in it. And yet, feeling that hunger awakened, I was secretly glad. I began to think of a new baby as an escape. This would spare me the difficulty of fighting that daily battle to do my job well and prove to others that I could do it.

A weird obsession took over. I started composing possible speeches to my department chair. Perhaps I should try the cavalier approach: "Well, you know, these things happen!" Or maybe the detailed, scientific explanation: "It must have been those antibiotics that suppressed the effect of the pill." Or perhaps the blunt approach would be best: "You know what? I'm glad, as this will give me an excuse for a graceful exit from this good-for-nothing job!" Meanwhile, I obsessively noted subtle changes in my body, clandestinely inspecting my breasts about twenty-five times a day, wondering if it could be true, hoping it was, wanting the inescapable complications of it all. In a spasm of breathless irrationality, I even went out and bought a pregnancy test. It was negative. Well, maybe I took it too early, I thought.

But then, my period came, right on time. And I felt relieved. It was not yet, I concluded in calm and dignified mental tones, the Right Time. I really did have to give my professional work more of a chance. I wanted my son to grow up a little bit more before having a sibling. Yes, this was best. But still I puzzled over why I had experienced what seemed like convincing symptoms. Could it have been psychosomatic? My body's way of fulfilling a semiconscious wish to just give up and get out of my job? A cowardly reaction on my part, if true. But finally I concluded that my body was probably not doing anything unusual at all; I was simply paying attention for once to a hormonal routine I usually ignored.

Once I had finished marveling at my own silliness, one thing remained: where before I hadn't been absolutely sure, now I knew that I definitely wanted another child. Making an emergency space for one in my addled mind convinced me that I deeply desired to make a real space for one soon. When I told Ron about this, he needed no convincing at all. "You know I want more kids!" was his matter-of-fact reaction. Perhaps, then, this little practice run was a matter of body wisdom more than psychic foolishness, a hunger cry from within.

The Reckless Yes

So the fitting number of months have passed, and now we permit ourselves to speak the Yes, with words and with our bodies, deliberately and surely.

When I went off the pill I started listening to my body again. I attended to its rhythms and subtle shifts. On the third day of my first non-chemically controlled period, I had a horrible headache all day, the kind of headache that feels as if some tank of brain chemicals had bottomed out and my brain was shriveling up inside my skull. I took Ron's old college textbook for human biology off the shelf and found a helpful chart showing that this is not too far from what actually happens: the levels of both estrogen and progesterone plummet just before the onset of menstruation. This explains the terrible upheaval some women feel in their bodies at this time. The "progesterone plummet" can be fast and severe, making it tough for the body's systems to cope gracefully. Then, the levels of both hormones bottom out during the bleeding stage of the cycle. The resulting headache for me on that bottom-out day was a rotten distraction, but it occurred to me that I might better think of it as a kind of ritual emptying, a low point on a curve that could now rise to buoy something completely new and uncontrolled, something outside myself and my ability to direct.

This is why I am fond of this moment of the Yes: it is reckless.

Recklessness and fertility go together. The ancient Greeks knew this in the person of the crazy party god Dionysus. Recklessness is not, of course, always a good thing. Dionysus is also the god of drunkenness, excess, even violence. For some people, the act that engenders conception is most unfortunately reckless, as one or both partners say "yes" only to heated flesh in the moment, or to some confused desire for acceptance and love, and not to the potential consequences. And when there is violence, then there is no Yes at all, but only a male assent to misogynistic violence and evil, and the life that results seems a cruelly ironic backlash at the destructive forces that initiated it. God have mercy.

But even when the decision to have a child is a fully conscious one, it is not without recklessness. Ron and I know very well that another child is laughably impractical. We are both semicompetent professionals, with enough investment in education to strongly motivate us both toward career-minded decisions. Since our two children will both be in school in a couple of years, the careerist thing to do would be to wait out these two years with our current one-main-income arrangement (mine) and then move ahead full steam on parallel career tracks. Moreover, since we are committed to religious education for our children—a soberingly expensive prospect— another child would increase our financial burden for education alone by 50 percent. Combined with the longer "wait" time until the kids are in school and the reduced income during that time, another child is, financially speaking, a mistake.

And it's not just money. The slow track is hard not because we're so ambitious for career advancement, but because there are so many things we love to do that we have set aside for a season because our children need our time and energy. When I think of all the music I can't play, all the books I can't read, all the exercise I'm definitely not getting, I often drift toward self-pity and sometimes despair. I would never make a different choice. I never resent what I give to Miriam and Jacob. But I do keenly feel the loss of what I give up. Another child will mean more of this, for a longer time.

And besides all that, our house isn't quite big enough, either. We're filling up the bedrooms now. Where would we put a nursery?

Well, one can duly note these contingencies, listing them off in late-evening sessions with pencils and yellow legal pads. But pragmatism hardly captures my fancy. Instead, I find the recklessness irresistibly alluring. I greet it with a sense of rebellion against all that is practical and sensible, about me, about anything. My usual taste for control and closure makes this recklessness all the more delicious. It is a relief from myself. I take pleasure now in surrendering to the unknown.

Human beings must begin in recklessness. Even the most carefully planned and intensely wanted baby must begin with the parents saying Yes to something they cannot control. I wonder if creation is always like this. I wonder if God felt reckless when he spoke the first creative word. The Judeo-Christian notion of divine creation through fiat and the majestically ordered poem of creation in Genesis hardly suggest recklessness, but I like to think of God covering his eyes with one hand, cringing with the wildness of it all, and saying, "Let there be . . ." Then, the cautious parting of the fingers, the divine eye peeping through, a reverberant whisper declaring, almost in surprise: "That's good!"

This giving over of the self to whatever happens, this poising of the self for possibility—I could not relish it if it weren't for the ultimate trust I have in the sense of this universe, in the compassion and power of the Creator, in God's sharing of hunger and promise of joy, somehow, sometime. This is not, for me, recklessness in a void. The giving over of my tiny helm is a chance to drift on something larger than myself. So I say now: streams and patterns of cosmic flow, chance and chaos, Providence and Divine Love—now *you* decide. I merely open myself, and wait.

SCREWTAPE INSTRUCTS
SCRAPETOOTH

(From beliefnet.com)

My dear Scrapetooth,

You may wonder at receiving a communication from some-one of my Abysmal Seniority. The truth is, I was on an errand in the Second Circle and happened to pass by the student notice boards, where the new patient assignments are posted. Permit me to congratulate you on being assigned a television anchorman. I look forward to seeing what you do with him. The task is significant and complicated enough to have attracted considerable attention Below; you may consider it a chance to show your paces and impress prominent diabolical figures, among whom I number myself. You may think I refer to the importance of tempting a subject who, if properly turned, can help mislead, confuse, and ultimately recruit to our side the many millions of additional souls in his viewing audi-ence. Not so! Or, at least, not primarily. One can attain bril-liant successes and deep professional satisfaction through the corruption of a completely private person. (And one can fail abjectly . . . ah, that miserable, delicious Wormwood! But I digress.) What makes this particular task truly noteworthy is the combination of a private person of limited gifts with a powerful and outsized public persona. Purely from a gastronomic perspective, the potential rewards are awesome. Such twistings and turnings of insecurity and self-justification, such excellent and succulent depths of self-deception! Some of us already have begun to salivate. Do not disappoint us. Many interesting tactical choices lie before you—for instance, whether to let your man become progressively more entranced with the power and influence of his position, and more committed to enhancing that status at any cost, or whether instead to whip him with the sense that what he does is "only" journalism, a game of surfaces and hurried deadlines, and let him lose himself in reveries of someday doing something more "serious." The first strategy will gradually render him unbearably arrogant and unreachable by normal scruples. The second will prevent genuine engagement with the task before him, with the attendant career stagnation, frustration, and hostility. Either dish can be satisfying; it is really a matter of personal taste.

Feel free to call upon me any time. We have not met much, but I am still a senior devil and as such command my small degree of influence Down Here.

Your affectionate third cousin twice removed,

Screwtape

My dear Scrapetooth,

You ask how I come by what you call my special knowledge of TV journalists, yours in particular. Dear boy, I hope I did not mislead. I have no direct knowledge of the creature who is under your supervision. I merely extended to him the observations I have made of the hapless members of his profession who have found their way here before him. (A habit you ought to practice, by the way. Relegation of the individual case to a general category based on under-informed assumption is an essential skill to master if you wish to descend the ladder of Nether Administration.) But back to my supposed expertise regarding your patient. The explanation is simple. Novice devils are not generally aware that here and there in the nether regions—specifically, in portions of the Fourth, Fifth, and Eighth Circles, on the southerly side—it is possible to pick up a steady stream of terrestrial television signals. You would be surprised how many devils while away their time between shifts decoding and imbibing these emissions, especially the all-news channels. They are not as satisfying to the appetite as the direct draughts of human fear, anguish, and confusion that we enjoy in the course of our duties, but they serve well as a snack between meals and as a reminder of those ultimate pleasures. We are led to believe that television reception is even better in the Other Place but that its denizens do not share our interest in it.

My direct impressions of your man have been—of necessity—superficial, but a few thoughts present themselves. He reads the news slowly and sonorously, plainly enamored of his own voice. This affords you opportunities to feed his vanity, encouraging him to concentrate more on the figure he cuts doing his job than on the satisfactions of the job itself. And that is essential if you are to block any chance of his striving to use his influential position for good deeds. The more you can enhance his feeling that he enjoys special status, the likelier you will be, in any given situation, to persuade him that on this occasion it is better to keep his powder dry—after all, he is a very important man; he ought to husband his influence and save it for a time when it will do the most good. With a little work on your part, you can make sure that that time will never come.

Your cousin,
Screwtape

My dear Scrapetooth,

You and your patient gave me quite a scare yesterday evening. Watching him host his special in-depth program on the future of public assistance, I was distressed to hear him delve at length into questions of what human creatures at the moment are pleased to call "ethics." At one particularly alarming moment—I need not remind you of it, surely—he turned those well-known deep-set eyes directly toward the camera, furrowed that striking brow, and asked, "We know this will balance the budget. But is it the right thing to do?"

For an awful second I feared you had already lost control

of your subject. I feared for your continued well-being. Had the man developed the habit—the rare, noxious habit—of weighing the morality of everything that passed his lips? The phenomenon has been known to occur, even among journalists. Generally it means some devil has relaxed his vigilance in elementary matters. Over the last few generations we have been highly successful in limiting the damage done by the popularity of ethical codes in private life—the humans' unaccountable attraction to, if not success at, being truthful, faithful, loving, and so forth. We have done this by gradually inculcating the unexamined idea that those codes must be interpreted differently, at any rate less literally, when one is going about the business that furnishes one's livelihood. How many exemplary cases have I seen who, while committed firmly to the Enemy's service at home and on the weekends, spend their working hours telling the untruths known fashionably today as "spin" or advancing policies or projects whose likely bad effects they studiously avoid thinking about on the grounds that an employee's foremost ethical obligation is to advance the interests of the company! What a surprise for them when they discover their real home is with us. Journalists—did you wonder when I would return to the business at hand?—suffer a special, rather subtle case of this confusion, and as a result they must be handled with delicacy. As a rule they do not simply suspend their moral codes while working, but, rather, consider their work to be subject to an ethical code of its own that is different from the everyday one but just as rigorous. A primary feature of this professional code is the insistence that the journalist should not think too much about the likely consequences of publishing his story or about whom it will hurt or help. This is called being objective. It is asserted that a focus on the (unknowable) consequences of reporting a news story would make it impossible for stories to be reported fairly or effectively.

I cannot claim that this potentially useful element of your patient's professional formation is the work of our Research Department. No, it bears some of the Enemy's hallmarks—I believe he has some notion of getting the creatures to focus their attention on the parts of their lives they can control and de-emphasizing those they cannot. Nonetheless it is a tool we have been able in many cases to turn to our purposes. The first step is to heighten the patient's sense that, since his work falls under the jurisdiction of its own code of ethics, it exists in some real way separate from ordinary life and its "ordinary" rules. The second step is to enhance that feeling of being outside the rules until it begins to color all his non-work life as well.

I have known cases where this sense of journalistic detachment was so successfully advanced that the patient declined in private life to make contributions to charitable causes, to perform routine community obligations such as volunteering for his children's school events, to develop opinions on the great political issues of his day—even, in one case, to vote in national elections. All to maintain the status of journalistic observer in its most pristine form! This is excellent; this is ideal.

So you can imagine my concern on hearing your patient express, first, a direct ethical concern about the contents of his story, and second, an implied solidarity with ordinary citizens' interest in the morality of public programs. My concern gnaws at me; it pains me. I await with tense eagerness any explanation you can offer.

Your very impatient, very distant cousin,

Screwtape

My dear Scrapetooth,

The calm audacity of your reply amazes me. You assert in unruffled tones (a trifle too unruffled, in truth, to address someone of my Depth in the administration) that you have the situation well under control. The man, you say, is not becoming moral at all; he is merely going with the fashion. Yes, among the humans of today, a dip into morality is now considered the latest thing! The temper of the times, you say, is against the journalistic presumption of objectivity; in the patient's city and in the circles within which he moves, not so much his colleagues but his confidential sources and high official contacts, one's credibility is enhanced by being "born again." You claim to have impressed laboriously on your patient's mind the disadvantage he suffers from not being thus newly "born again," his lack of access to the inner circles of power, their shared language, their bible study classes and men's fellowships and prayer breakfasts. You point with pride to your success in keeping him away from any notion that he might actually join this world by converting. Rather, under the influence of the drumming envy and discontent you inflicted, he conceived the notion of presenting himself as a sort of morally struggling, questing figure—not just different from his journalistic colleagues but in active contrast to them.

If this tale of yours is true, I must express my admiration. I have not seen so neat a spot of moral jujitsu since an episode in my own early career, when, faced by a patient being importuned to embrace the Enemy's service, I realized that a pretended conversion for social gain would mire my man in a lifetime of hypocrisy while also giving him endless hours of fear and anxiety lest he be found out. It sounds as if you have had a similar brainstorm. In allowing your patient to salt his broadcasts with moral-sounding but empty verbal gestures, a sort of surface moral vocabulary, all for the purpose of signaling his membership in a select peer group, you are using the Enemy's dearest tools in the service of mere snobbism. This is delightful, and it promises more gains in future. Moral postures struck for the purpose of keeping up with the fashion are not necessarily disqualifying for the Enemy—he, our Intelligence Service tells us, clings in such cases to the chance that outward habit will inculcate inward purpose—but there is no doubt that they are at least initially corrupting. And moral postures struck in the plain sight of several million news viewers, most of whom will take the posturing at face value, exert a uniquely corrosive effect on the man's other professional values.

But how can we be sure in the long run that the surface posturing will not become the real thing? For that matter, my dear Scrapetooth, how can I be sure that this explanation on your part is true and is not just a highly original way to cover an impending disaster? No doubt we will know soon enough: I, for one, intend to watch assiduously whether the patient's moral posturing helps his immediate career prospects, as he expects it to, and what use he makes of any advancement. A large new dose of responsibility has been known unaccountably to sober up its holder and turn him to serious thoughts, of the sort that endanger our project. On the other hand, it can serve merely as a bigger and faster car with which he can drive himself where he was going anyway.

As I compose these sentences I note a broadcast announcement that your man will soon anchor an hourlong special on how ordinary citizens can combat the moral vacuity of everyday life. It looks as if his, and your, career strategy is paying off smartly: he is being given a chance to fill a journalistic niche as Moral Philosopher. How will he handle this initial foray—with continued superficiality or, perish the idea, with sincerity and thoughtfulness? The stakes, my dear Scrapetooth, are high for you also.

Your urgently interested cousin,
Screwtape

Well, well, my newly promoted colleague,
my dear, esteemed Scrapetooth,

I cannot be the first to congratulate you—others in the structure of authority Down Here are too quick for that. But I hope I may add my voice in admiration for the way in which your patient acquitted himself. And so soon after his elevation to the moral-philosopher role he craved, with the assignment of hosting a series of taped specials on moral conundrums! It is true he is not safe in Our House yet—that must await his departure from the mortal world. Still, certain actions taken during the taping of his latest show point him firmly in our direction. It would require a real contravention of what he is pleased to call the Moral Law for him to end up traveling any other way.

It was delicious, was it not? He had just gone on air to engage two pundits and a research scientist in a discussion of what the government could do to help families whose children suffer from some dread disease. (I forget the particulars already; physical suffering is always welcome, but its details bore us.) Earlier in the show he had convened another panel of families involved, tragic figures struggling to save their children from agonized untimely death. One of these desperate parents after going off the air had asked him to broker an introduction between themselves and the second panel's research scientist—nothing dramatic, nothing to catch a devil's eye, just one of those tiny insidious actions from which some good might result. And what was our patient's response?

He forgot to do it. He had no particular reason to make or not to make this small connection; the thing merely slipped his mind.

Such a result, my dear Scrapetooth, testifies to your alert presence at your patient's elbow and to the finesse with which you had previously worked him over. It proves beyond a doubt that your analysis of his moral state all along was correct. The honors now being heaped upon you are well deserved, and your future success seems guaranteed. As you progress Downward I sincerely hope you will spare a thought for those of us who offered you advice along the way. And one other thing: your continued close relationship with your patient ought to put you in a good position to recommend guests for future specials. Tell me, if a senior devil such as myself—experienced, authoritative, photogenic—were to obtain the necessary clearances from Below, do you think your patient would be interested in putting him on TV?

Your attentive and sympathetic third cousin,

Screwtape

COLUMBINE, KUDZU,
AND A COLT .45

(From *Sojourners*)

We were drinking coffee in the prison employee break room when Mark and Sam started comparing their childhood terrors. They both grew up with alcoholic dads. They both were subjected to a daily barrage of insults, hits, cursings, and cruelty. Sometimes they escaped by running or hiding, only to watch a pet or sibling or mother receive the blows. They learned that they both were taken with their dads to the same bootlegger tucked away in a mountain hollow. They swapped stories of fights with fists, bottles, knives, and guns. They pointed to scars. They felt lucky to have survived at all. And what did they survive with?

Mark stood in blue uniform with gold stripes on his collar and black weapons hanging from his belt. He's a sergeant and earned badges as an expert marksman. Mark speaks with delight about shooting birds out of trees, watching the feathers scatter to the ground. Some days, he says, he just wants to kill something—anything. Just feels the urge. Loud noises still make him jump at night. He grabs his Colt .45 under his pillow to investigate the sound. He never answers his door without a gun.

Sam sat in a blue-striped shirt. He is a prison counselor. He does not own a gun. He walks away when a movie becomes too violent. Sometimes he likes to walk in the woods at night and call out to screech owls. Just feels the urge. Loud noises still make him jump. He will grab his glasses at the bedside to investigate the sound. He never goes to his door without his glasses.

Violence does not always beget violence. Gentleness does not always beget gentleness. Ask parents. The roads our children take are often wildly divergent. They defy explanation by even the most discerning minds. The same stimuli do not produce the same results. How do we explain it?

The first garden had the tree of the knowledge of good and evil. We have been chomping its fruit with equal portions of horror and delight ever since. It seems we cannot savor good without sampling evil. "Columbine" used to refer to a beautiful mountain wildflower. Now it conjures up a national tragedy of teens killing teens. What happened? Bad parenting? Neglectful teachers? Easy access to guns? The media? Our love affair with violence? Sin? Satan?

Hannah Arendt dubbed the undramatic way that we live with absurdity and call it normality "the banality of evil." Evil, it appears, is as common as kudzu and as predictable as the evening news.

In Billie Letts' novel *Where the Heart Is*, Lexie asks her friend Novalee how she will ever explain the sexual abuse done to her children by her boyfriend. She wonders what to tell her kids about the evil visited upon them. Novalee answers, "Tell them that our lives can change with each breath we take. . . . Tell them to let go of what's gone because men like Roger never win. And tell them to hold on like hell to what they've got—each other, and a mother who would die for them. . . . Tell them we've all got meanness in us . . . but tell them that we have some good in us too. And the only thing worth living for is the good. That's why we've got to make sure we pass it on."

In the end isn't it the mystery of goodness that most baffles and amazes us? Isn't it the incredulity of good that astonishes our life together? Columbines are still flowers that spring up wild in the mountains. God's still on the earth and all is wild with the world. Goodness still happens.

THE DERELICT CROSS

(From *The Christian Century*)

Over the years I have accumulated dozens of crosses. I purchased quite a few of them myself, such as the crudely poured brass cross I bought from a young girl in Ethiopia, or the small golden one I found in a shop in East Jerusalem. Others have been gifts.

When I attended the Niobrara Convocation, a gathering of Lakota people in South Dakota, I admired the distinctive cross worn by members of that body. Made from stamped nickel, each cross hung from an elaborately beaded necklace that incorporated the red, white, and blue shield of the Episcopal Church. Noting my covetousness, a native woman lifted her cross off her neck and placed it around mine. "You take it," she said. "I'm not even sure I believe in it anymore."

Every cross has its own story. Recently a friend brought me a small standing cross from Ireland that was made from pressed sod. From the front it looks like tooled leather, but if you turn it over you can still catch a whiff of Irish bog. I placed it in the library, next to a flat green cross cut from an old slate shingle that was removed from the roof of a church I once served.

None of these is the cross that is currently troubling me, however. That one is about six inches high, made of plain dark wood, with a thin silver body hanging on it. The body is tacked to the cross by three tiny nails, one each in the hands and one for both of the feet. The small head is down and the mouth is open. It looks like something from the 1960s, which is when I first visited the Cistercian monastery in Conyers, Georgia. I was a new Christian and I wanted a cross to hang in my dorm room. The young monk in the gift shop helped me pick it out, along with a couple of books by Thomas Merton and a loaf of brown Trappist bread.

The cross hung on my wall until my graduation from college. Then it went into a box that I carted from place to place for the next thirty years. When I cleaned out the attic earlier this summer I unearthed it, along with some old scrapbooks and a pair of bell-bottomed jeans. I tried to put it in a box for the Salvation Army, but my hand would not let go of it. Meanwhile, the metal loop at the top has disappeared so that I could not hang it on the wall even if I wanted to. What does one do with a derelict cross?

I could not decide, so I set it in a clear spot on my dresser. The next day I needed the clear spot for a stack of bills, so I put the crucifix on top of them. Underneath the upraised arms of the small body, I could see how many frequent flyer miles I earned last month for charging groceries, gas, new shoes, and some theater tickets to my American Express card. After I paid the bills, I needed the space for some papers from my world religions class, so I put the crucifix on them. When I reached for the stack the next morning I realized that Jesus had just spent the night on a color copy of a Tibetan Buddhist sand mandala.

At first this seemed irreverent to me, to keep shuffling a sacred symbol across the debris on my dresser. Shouldn't I put it in some dedicated space where it would not rub up against such unholy junk? But then it occurred to me that I had unwittingly invented a sacrament. Hardly a day goes by that I do not handle this cross, deciding where to put it and noticing how it changes whatever lies beneath it. One day it sits on pictures of my godchildren, the next on a tin of chocolates from Maxim's. Sometimes the small body confers a blessing, but more often it constitutes a judgment. Whose hands have ever been so empty? Whose purposes have ever been so pure?

Lately I have begun to wish for a different symbol to emulate. I think about commissioning a small statue of Peter, half in the water and half out, with Jesus holding him by the scruff of his neck. Or perhaps a silver pendant of Mary sitting at Jesus' feet, while Martha threatens her with a wooden spoon. If I could look at one of those on a regular basis, then I might rest easier in my skin, because I know how to sink and I know how to sit. It is dying I am no good at, as my movable cross reminds me every day.

I remain grateful that Jesus did not say, "Be me." He said, "Follow me," but when I imagine a Peter or a Mary on my dresser I realize what I would lose. Neither of them would blink an eye at my check stubs or grocery lists. They were as immersed in such things as I am, and while they may have made better choices than I, we understand each other. They do not want me to be anyone but me.

But that small body on the cross seems to have other ideas. Having let go of everything that anchored him to this reality, he is the open doorway to a far richer one. I am free to walk through him or to stay where I am, but either way he never stops whispering to me to take the next step. I don't understand him. He seems to think that "me" is too limited a concern.

"I became human for you," he whispered to Meister Eckhart more than half a millennium ago. "If you do not become God for me, you do me wrong." I do not expect ever to solve the mystery of the cross, but I do take heart in the unlikely good news that the cross has already solved me.

THINGS SEEN AND UNSEEN

(From boundless.org)

A woman in a white coat walked into the room and flipped on the fluorescent lights, jarring my wife awake. Bethany had been asleep for about half an hour—the longest nap she had managed all day. Though the doctor had ordered her to get plenty of sleep, nurses kept coming in every few minutes to take her temperature and blood pressure.

The day before, we were invited to lunch at a Thai restaurant. When we returned home, Bethany was bothered by a cramp in her side. Blaming the food, she laid down in bed. But after four hours of increasing pain, we left for the emergency room, thinking that it might be appendicitis. We were right, and after a few hours her appendix was removed with no complications (other than some nausea, which, when combined with Thai food, is especially unpleasant).

All this would have been quite routine, except that Bethany was fifteen weeks pregnant. As it turned out, the timing was good: a younger, less-established baby might be at risk for miscarriage, while an older, larger baby would make it hard to get at the appendix. Our baby's heartbeat was monitored both before and after surgery, and rather than putting Bethany to sleep, a local anesthetic was used. The one redeeming part of this experience came before the surgery, when Bethany's appendix was examined by ultrasound and we were able to see our baby cruising around his amniotic home. (I say "his"—we asked the technician not to tell us, but it looked like a he to us.)

We were amazed at our baby's development at only four months of age, when Bethany was hardly "showing" at all and could feel none of his movements. There on the ultrasound screen we could see clearly his head and skull, spine and ribs, arms and legs, hands and feet. Even a tiny heart was beating—at a rate of 160, to be exact. We watched in wonder as he kicked, fluttered, and twirled about, quite oblivious to his mother's condition.

For new fathers, especially, it's difficult to fathom that inside your wife is a whole little person waiting to be introduced to the world. The ultrasound technician printed out several photos for us to keep, and later—as I sat in an empty waiting room at 2:00 A.M. taking advantage of the free cappuccino machine—I looked at the photos and wondered how the little guy was doing about now. In one picture, his mouth was open and it looked like he was trying to say something. Above his head, the technician had typed "Hello!"

. . .

It was now the evening after surgery, and Bethany needed rest more than anything. There were two television sets in every room, and Bethany's roommate watched talk shows all day. While she struggled to sleep, Jerry Springer's guests screamed at each other. By midnight, after Jay Leno's monologue, the television was finally turned off. Bethany at last fell asleep. I sank into my chair, next to her bed, and closed my eyes.

Then the lights came on. Bethany squinted under the glare, looking disoriented. The doctor stood over her, shuffling through some papers on a clipboard. "How are you feeling tonight?"

"Tired," Bethany answered. I wished the doctor could take a hint and leave us in peace.

The woman announced that she was an obstetrician. After reviewing Bethany's history and asking a few questions, she scribbled something down on her clipboard and stated that she was ordering a routine test for tomorrow morning.

"What kind of test?" Bethany asked, still half asleep.

"An Alpha-Feto Protein screen," she explained. We asked what it would test for, and why we should have it now, rather than later in the pregnancy during a visit with our own doctor.

"Well, it can tell you if the fetus has neural-tube defects, Down Syndrome, or if the brain is not complete. Then, if something is wrong with the fetus, you can decide to terminate the pregnancy while it is still a safe, legal time to do so."

I looked at Bethany—she appeared to be as uncomfortable as I was. This was a Christian hospital, affiliated with an evangelical denomination. Being told that we might want to abort our child was the last thing we expected, or wanted to argue about under the circumstances. I tried to deflect the question. "We've talked about the different tests available with our own doctor, and we aren't going to have that one."

"Now is the ideal time. If you wait until you are further along, it might be too late," she continued coldly. "The hospital strongly recommends the test, because parents might hold us liable if they have a disabled child. They will ask, 'Why didn't you warn us?'"

"But we're not going to have an abortion—under any circumstance. It wouldn't matter what disabilities our baby had. We're not going to have the test."

"Well, I can't force you to have any test if you don't want it," the doctor shot back, and left as quickly as she had come. Bethany started to cry.

My tears came later, after Bethany had fallen back asleep, when I picked up the ultrasound photos again. In one, nearly every bone in his arm and hand was strikingly visible. He seemed to be waving for the camera—shamelessly soaking up the limelight even at such a young age. "Hello!"

I wished the doctor were there, so I could ask her, *what is this a picture of?*

Even science alone verifies that it is a human being. At the moment of conception, sperm and egg unite to form something entirely different—a genetically complete, self-determining organism, entirely unique and distinct from its parents. The mere presence of that newly conceived baby—far too small to be seen except through a high-powered microscope—is enough to trigger a complete readjustment of his mother's hormone levels, preparing her to nurture the new life growing inside her womb. Left to normal biological processes, this organism will develop continuously from zygote, to fetus, to infant, to toddler, to teenager, and so on, with no substantial change to its being.

But science cannot tell us whether this human being has any intrinsic value. If we aren't happy with the baby we've conceived, if a test shows that there's "something wrong" with him, if he's going to have a low IQ, if he has a terminal defect and will die within a few years anyway—wouldn't it be better to "terminate the pregnancy"?

The Bible tells us that man is created in the image and likeness of God. This is not a scientific statement, but a poetic one. The image of God cannot be observed under a microscope or detected by an ultrasound scan—but it can be expressed in a poem.

In a hymn to the Creator, the psalmist writes:

Thou didst form my inward parts;
Thou didst weave me in my mother's womb.
I will give thanks to Thee, for I am fearfully and
    wonderfully made. . . .

Psalm 139:13–14

If this poetry can be believed, each human person is a masterpiece of God's craftsmanship. Life is a gift to be received joyfully; it is not a creation of man, and we have no right to destroy it.

If each person we encounter bears the divine image, none should be exploited or used. Each of us—irrespective of size, age, or intelligence—is unique, irreplaceable, and invaluable. The only response to a human person is love.

If we are each created in the image of God, whatever we do to another person, we ultimately do to God himself. Jesus said, "Truly I say to you, to the extent that you did it to one of these brothers of mine, even the least of them, you did it to me" (Matthew 25:40).

Jesus made it clear that this is especially true of children. "And He called a child to Himself and set him before them, and said, 'Truly I say to you, . . . whoever receives one such child in My name receives Me'" (Matthew 18:2, 5).

The Apostle Paul writes that faith is "the assurance of things hoped for, the evidence of things not seen." But faith is not only about things unseen. There is another kind of faith—the faith to see, hear, and understand what is right in front of our noses.

For the heart of this people has become dull,
And with their ears they scarcely hear,
And they have closed their eyes;

Lest they should see with their eyes,

And hear with their ears,

And understand with their heart and return,

And I should heal them.

Matthew 13:15

To see the world around us for what it truly is, we must open our eyes—not just the literal eyes of our heads, but the poetic eyes of our hearts. To be healed is to be made whole. Head and heart, science and poetry, reason and faith—these are not supposed to be opposites, but complementary ways of seeing reality. They are reconciled in the unity of truth.

Just past 1:00 A.M., tired but unable to sleep, I tried my best to curl up comfortably on a small plastic chair next to Bethany's hospital bed. Looking again at my baby's ultrasound pictures, I tried to picture clearly in my mind's eye what was so roughly suggested in the grainy black and white photos. I saw the delicate tapestry of flesh and blood and bone, woven together in the secret depths of my wife's body. I saw an irreplaceable person, never to be repeated again on this earth. I saw an embodied soul who will live forever, and for whom I am eternally responsible. I saw the visible image of the invisible God.

WALTER WANGERIN, JR.

ONE MAN ON A TRACTOR
FAR AWAY

(From *Christianity Today*)

I own a John Deere 5000 series farm tractor. It pulls at the power of forty horses, more than enough to handle the work I do on twenty-four acres: light plowing and disking. I drag timber from the woods to cut and split for firewood; I mow the broader fields, stretch fence, chip tree limbs, grade the ground, and haul—all with my little Deere. After having lived for more than a decade in the confinement of the inner city, to me this machine represents breadth and the breathing of my spirit. It is perfectly suited to the cultivation of our modest crops, berry bushes, hickory and walnut trees, strawberry hills, scattered stands of apple trees, a sizable vegetable garden.

The tractor allows and empowers my personal participation in the rhythms of the natural world. I can plant and pick, harrow and harvest generous crops in season. To me, my tractor seems a heroic thing.

But in the field of farm tractors, my Deere is as small as they run. Even if you're not a farmer, you've seen tractors twice and thrice the power of mine commonly plowing the dark Midwestern soil. And on the larger tracts, you've seen modern behemoths cut swaths as wide as avenues through dustier fields, wearing double tires on every wheel, pulling several gangs of plows and harrows, while the operator sits bunkered in an air-conditioned cab, watching the tracks of his tires in a television monitor.

Me, I take the weather on my head. I mow at a width of six feet. And mine is but a two-bottom plow.

Nevertheless, as small as my tractor is, smaller still was the first tractor purchased by my father-in-law, Martin Bohlmann, in the late 1940s when his daughter Ruthanne was six years old.

A Sad Elemental Yearning

When I was a young man, I once sat down to supper with the farmer and his family in their spacious kitchen. Outside, the evening air was warm, rich, and loamy. Jonquils and daffodils were in bloom, the tulip buds about to pop. It was nearly Easter. I had come to court Ruthanne, the farmer's daughter.

There were eight of us at the table, though it could accommodate fifteen at least. Martin and Gertrude had borne fourteen children. They buried one in infancy and now had watched nearly all the others leave for college.

The farmer bowed his head. We prayed and began to eat. Potatoes and vegetables had been raised in the kitchen garden. Popcorn, too. Milk came from their own cows. There had been a time when the hog had been hung up on a chilly autumn morning and butchered in the barn door to become cracklings, hams, chops, sausages, lard. The Bohlmanns didn't own the land they worked or the house they slept in. They rented. They never paid income tax, since their annual income never approached a taxable figure. For them it was a short distance from the earth to their stomachs and back to earth again. "Thanne" remembers when they had no plumbing.

We consumed our supper mostly in silence. Then, at the end of the meal, Martin put a toothpick in the corner of his mouth, read a brief devotion, pushed back his chair, stood up, and walked outside. I followed as far as the porch. In twilight the farmer, clad in clean coveralls, strolled westward into the field immediately beyond the house. He paused. He stood in silhouette, the deep-green sky framing his body with such precision that I could see the toothpick twiddling in his lips. His hair was as stiff and wild as a thicket, his nose majestic.

Slowly, Martin knelt down on one knee. He gathered some soil in his right hand and squeezed and sifted the dirt through his fingers to the palm of his left. Suddenly he brought both hands to his face and sniffed. He switched the toothpick. He touched the tip of his tongue to the earth. Then he rose again, softly clapping his two hands clean and slipping them behind the bib of the coveralls. He stood there, Martin Bohlmann, gazing across the field, black as iron in the gloaming, his elbows forming the joints of folded wings—and I thought, *How peaceful! How completely peaceful is this man.*

It caused in me a sort of sadness, a nameless elemental yearning.

Buying a Sturdy Servant

Martin purchased that first tractor of his—a John Deere exactly as green as mine but smaller and less powerful—at the only price he could afford, something less than $200. *Billig,* he judged the sale, German for "cheap," which in his mouth meant "Such a deal!" He bought the tractor used from one of his neighbors. The machine wasn't even two years old but it had kept stalling. In the barnyard, in the field, it would quit, then refuse to produce a spark for starting again, however hard the poor man cranked it. The neighbor figured he was selling aggravation.

Martin, on the other hand, was buying a sturdy servant, not only with cash but also with his character: less than $200 bought the cold equipment; patience and peace bought time to examine it with a complete attention, his mind untroubled, undivided; and mother-wit brought the tractor to life again.

In those days tractors used a magneto generator. My father-in-law opened it and discovered a loose washer inside. The washer had shifted whenever the tractor bumped over rough ground, shorting the coils and killing the engine.

Martin simply removed that washer. Thereafter he had a dependable tractor for as long as ever he farmed. It was there when I came courting Ruthanne. It was there when he finally retired at the age of seventy and was forced to auction off his farming equipment.

Quiet Obedience

My father-in-law was born in the early twentieth century. His relationship to the earth, therefore, was established long before society developed its ever more complex technologies for separating human creatures from the rest of creation.

Throughout his young manhood, farming was the labor of muscle and bone, hoof and hand. The very first successful gasoline tractor wasn't produced until 1892. In 1907 there were a mere six hundred tractors in the whole of the United States.

Thanne still remembers the years before her father purchased that first John Deere, when he plowed behind draft horses, Prince and Silver, steady beasts with hooves the size of a little girl's head. Often she was sent to lead them to water. And this is why she remembers the time and the chore so well: it frightened the child to walk between two massive motors of rolling hide, her head below their necks. The quicker she went, the quicker they took their longer paces, until she thought she could never stop them, and they all would fly into the pond.

Her father, however, commanded them mutely with a gesture, a cluck, a tap of the bridle. Silent farmer. Silent, stolid horses. They were for him a living, companionable power. When they spent days plowing fields together, their wordless communication became community. The farmer never worked alone. He was never isolated. And if the dog ran beside them, then there were four who shared a certain peace beneath the sky, four who could read and obey the rhythms of creation, four creatures, therefore, who dwelt in communion with the Creator.

Horses plowed. Horses mowed. Horses pulled the rake that laid the alfalfa in windrows to dry—giving Martin's fields the long, strong lines of a darker green that looked like emotion in an ancient face.

And when the hay was dry, horses pulled a flat wagon slowly by the windrows while one man forked the hay up to another who stood on the wagon. That second man caught the bundles neatly with his own fork and flicked them into an intricate cross-arrangement on the wagon, building the hay tighter and higher, climbing his work as he did, climbing so high that when the horses pulled the wagon to the barn, the man on his haystack could stare dead-level into the second-story windows of the farmhouse. Then horses pulled the rope that, over a metal wheel, hoisted the hay to the loft in the barn.

Martin and his neighbors made hayricks of the overflow. They thatched the tops against rain and the snow to come. The work caused a gritty dust, and the dust caused a fearful itch on a summer's day. But the work and the hay—fodder for fall and the winter to come—were a faithful obedience to the seasons and the beasts, Adam and Eve responsible for Eden. Martin Bohlmann knew that.

He milked the cows before sunrise. There was a time when he sat on a stool with his cheek against their warm flanks in winter. Cows would swing their heads around to gaze at him. He pinched the teats in the joint of his thumb and squeezed with the rest of his hand, shooting a needle spritz into the pail between his feet. He rose. He lifted the full pail and sloshed its blue milk into the can; then he carried the cans, two by two, outside.

The winter air had a bite. His boots squeaked on stiff snow as he lugged the cans to the milk house. The dawn was gray at the eastern horizon, the white earth ghostly, the cold air making clouds at the farmer's nostrils—and someone might say that he, alone in his barnyard, was lonely. He wasn't, of course: he was neither lonely nor alone. His boots still steamed with the scent of manure; his cheek kept the oil of the cattle's flank; the milk and the morning were holy. They were manifestations of the Creator—and the work was Martin's peaceful obedience.

Ask What the Water Wants

Near the western boundary of my acreage, the land descends to a low draw through which my neighbor's fields drain their runoff water. When we first moved here, the only way I could get back to the woods and my writing studio was through that draw. But every spring the thaw and the rain turned it into a stretch of sucking mud.

In order to correct my problem, I laid a culvert east-and-west over the lowest section, then hired a man with a diesel earth shovel to dig a pond on the east side of the draw and pile that dirt over my culvert. I built a high bank, a dry pathway wide enough to take the weight of my tractor. I seeded it with grass, and the grass grew rich and green. Had God given us dominion over the earth? Well, I congratulated myself for having dominated this little bit of earth—until the following spring, when severe storms caused such thundering floods that the earth broke and my metal culvert was washed backward into the pond.

I tried again. I paid several students from the university to help me reset the culvert, redig and repile the earth upon it. I walled the mouth of the culvert with rock and stone in order to teach the water where to go. I reseeded the whole, and during the summer months I watched . . . as little runnels found their little ways under the culvert. By spring the runnels had scoured out caves, and the caves caused the culvert to slump, so that by autumn my draw had returned to its primeval state: mud.

When was it my father-in-law came to visit? I showed him my tractor. I showed him my fields. I asked him, as always, interminable questions, which he answered, as always, with two words and peace. My foolishness and all my concomitant anxieties were swallowed up—always, always—in the infinitude of Martin's patience. I showed him my failed culvert.

He said, "Take your time. You've got time. Ask the water what she wants, then give her a new way to do it."

Go to the Farmer

When it idles, my John Deere 5000 makes a low muttering sound. At full throttle it produces a commanding growl. But its voice is muffled, modern.

Martin's first tractor uttered that steady pop-pop-pop-pop which, when it crossed fields to the farmhouse, revealed the essential vastness of the earth and all skies.

Pop-pop-pop-pop! Look. Follow the sound with your eyes. See him moving slowly between solitary cottonwoods: one man on a tractor far away, creeping the low land under the white cumulus giants that people the blue sky. Look again and see yourself, for this is our true size upon the circle of the earth, as Isaiah declares: its inhabitants are like grasshoppers.

Does such diminishment crush you? Does it oppress or depress you, O Lofty Soul, to be reduced to a plant-eating insect? Are you rather more inclined to take power over your environment, heating it and cooling it according to your physical comfort, as if you were the standard of the weather? Encountering the world through car windows and television screens, O Citizen of the First World, thou art seldom wet, seldom sunstruck, never in darkness if you don't wish it, never a soul in communion with the soil, scarcely aware of the daily rhythms of creation, ever an alien on the earth, one who is alerted to her presence only when she turns around and dominates our pitiful dominion over her: hurricanes, tornadoes, blizzards, "acts," we say, "of God." Are you any less anxious for all your technologies of speed and swift communication with anyone but creation? Surely patience is not the virtue of e-mailing and cell-phoning. But are you more peaceful for all the distance now established between the earth and your stomach?

If Isaiah's description of your puling importance offends you, go out and garden. Plant things. Cultivate them. Pick them and eat them. Be forced to watch the weather. Try dependence on the creations of God at least as much as you depend on the inventions of humankind. Which would you rather obey? Which is it that loves you, even to the end?

Go, I suggest, to the farmer.

And if you cannot farm like him, watch him. Learn of him. Take your children to the places where people depend upon the earth: depend directly upon the earth, its produce, its benevolence, its living resource. Work with the farmer. Talk with him. Purchase some necessary food, whether fruit from the orchard, vegetables from the garden, eggs from the coop, or flowers. And find the farmer, if not in your own family, then through the networkings of your church or your denomination.

But I tell you from my own experience: even in the inner city, there are vacant lots waiting with eager longing for the clearing and the tilling of the children of God.

Reading the Weather Obediently

How peaceful! How completely peaceful was the man!

Once that observation filled me with a melancholy longing, since what Martin was, I was not. But that was more than thirty-three years ago.

In the meantime, I have come to know the man because I have been his son-in-law; and I have come to know his peace because I went out and joined myself to the rhythms of creation. However foolish and light my effort, I have a tractor. I do a little farming.

Martin Bohlmann was peaceful upon the land because he saw himself as small beneath the firmament. But his size was no diminishment. It was the beginning of wisdom. Martin was patient in creation because he believed himself to be an integral part of it all, a citizen of the universe, placed there by the wise Creator.

Faith and trust and farming were all the same to my father-in-law; therefore, he read the weather as humbly as he read the Bible, seeking what to obey. Martin was an obedient man, and his obedience was the source of his peace. Daily he did more than just read and interpret the rhythms of creation; even as Prince and Silver, heeding the farmer's mute commands, moved in communion with him, so did Martin, obeying the signs of the Creator, enter into communion with God eternal.

Here is peace: not in striving for greatness but in recognizing who is truly great. And this is peace: by sweet humility to do the will of the Creator. This is peace: to bear the image of God into creation.

And this is peace: to know and to believe Isaiah's words regarding grasshoppers.

> Have you not known? Has it not been told you from the beginning? It is he who sits above the circle of the earth, and its inhabitants are like grasshoppers; who stretches out the heavens like a curtain, and spreads them like a tent to dwell in. . . .
>
> Lift up your eyes on high and see: who created these? He who brings out their host by number, calling them all by name; by the greatness of his might, and because he is strong in power, not one is missing.
>
> (Isaiah 40:21–22, 26)

As long as he worked the earth, Martin enjoyed an unbroken communication with the one who sits above the circle of the earth. He never doubted that he had a personal purpose and a sacred worth.

And this is peace: to know that this communication with the Creator could not even be broken by death.

A Wonderful Joke

In 1994, at the age of ninety-four, Martin Bohlmann stuck a toothpick into his mouth, pushed back his chair from the supper table, stood up, and went outside. He strolled westward, into fields farther and farther beyond the land he rented—and there he paused. He stood a long while, his hands folded under the bib of his coveralls, growing ever darker in the twilight.

In his own good time the farmer knelt down and scooped up a handful of the black earth. Then, when at last he let the soil blow out of his hands again, it was himself that blew upon the wind, the dust of his human frame and the lightsome stuff of his spirit. Never had there been much distance between the earth and his heart and the earth again.

Martin died in a perfect peace.

And when his family gathered around the coffin to view his body once before the burial, we saw a joke, a wonderful joke. His hair was still, stiff and tangled as barbed wire, his nose a majesty thrust upward from the polished coffin; and his old eyes were closed. But into the corner of our father's mouth—to the deep distress of the mortician—someone had stuck a toothpick.

"IS SHE A BIBLE-THUMPER?"

I am sitting on the ninth floor of the Butler Library stacks, illegally eating a scone whose crumbs will probably sustain a generation of silverfish and reading a book about chocolate consumption in colonial New England. I'm in the middle of a detailed discussion of chocolate breakfast foods when I overhear two of my classmates, Y. and Z., chatting away. As graduate students are wont to do, they are gossiping about other graduate students, and I, of course, eavesdrop.

They are discussing the members of our nineteenth-century history seminar. "I thought I was going to throttle him," says Y., and it does not take too long for me to figure out that they are discussing R., an overbearing Harvard grad who plans to write a dissertation on the history of the polka dot. For the current seminar, he is writing about the polka dot during the era of the American Civil War. According to R., the Civil War transformed the status of the polka dot. His thesis is that "the Civil War liberated not only slaves, but fashion." At the start of the war, elegant ladies and foppish gents favored solids (and the occasional stripe). By the war's end, polka dots were all the rage. As R. sees it, this vogue for dots had something to do with the carnage of war: amid all the death, people wanted to affirm life, as symbolized by circles or, *mutatis mutandis,* polka dots.

"What gets me most," Y. is saying to Z., "is that he simply has no fashion sense. If you are going to write about the polka dot, you should make an effort to look sort of snazzy."

After analyzing R.'s collection of fraying wool sweaters, Y. moves on to F., who is writing about a more conventional subject: the fiscal policy of DeWitt Clinton, an early New York governor best remembered for building the Erie Canal. I am beginning to fidget when Y. finally comes around to the subject I've been anticipating: me.

"You're pretty good friends with that Lauren girl," Y. says to Z. This is true, although Z. and I are about as different as Felix and Oscar. Z. is leggy and elegant, always turning heads with her glossy black hair and the sexy gap between her two front teeth, whereas I only turn heads if I sneeze loudly, and my hair is so bland it doesn't even merit an adjective. She lives in a glam East Side apartment with her investment banking husband, fifteen-month-old son, and French au pair, while I subsist in my tiny grad school garret and wonder if I am responsible enough to adopt a cat. She studies New Deal elites and I study colonial Anglicans—she's about as interested in religion as I am in the finer points of antilock break systems. Nonetheless, she is my closest friend at Columbia, and I will have to confess to her later that I eavesdropped on her conversation with Y.

As Y. was saying: "You're pretty good friends with that Lauren girl. Is she some sort of fundamentalist Bible-thumper?"

I can barely suppress a giggle as I listen to Z. maneuver her way to a response. "Why do you ask?" asks Z.

"Well, there's her paper topic." Fair enough: I am writing a paper about the history of the Eucharist in nineteenth-century America. "And then, you know, she always seems to be quoting Saint Paul."

"I think *Bible-thumper* is something of a derisive term," says Z., and I, sitting with my chocolate book, want to cheer. "She is quite religious, though. I think she calls herself an evangelical. I don't think I've ever heard her call herself a Bible-thumper. Or a fundamentalist." Then Z. changes the subject back to the polka dot boy, and she and Y. walk away, leaving me to munch my scone and look around for a Bible to thump.

Z. was right. I don't call myself a fundamentalist.

David Brooks wrote a cover story in the *Atlantic Monthly* about the differences between red America (Republican, meatloaf-eating, religious, heartland) and blue America (Democratic, cappuccino-sipping, hyper-educated, urban). The folks in red America don't know that you never drink cappuccino after noon; many of them don't even know what cappuccino is. "Many of us in blue America," confessed Brooks, "don't even know the difference between an evangelical and a fundamentalist."

Blue America has good reason to be perplexed about the differences between evangelicals and fundamentalists. The fact is, there are few hard and fast differences. Theologically, both groups affirm the central tenets of orthodox Protestantism, such as the authority of Scripture (though fundamentalists tend to emphasize literal interpretation, and the doctrine of biblical inerrancy is more central to fundamentalist identity). The real differences, which are easier to intuit than to document, have to do with sensibility. Fundamentalists tend more toward bold separation from the rest of American culture. They tend to be more suspicious of interfaith and cross-denominational conversations. Fundamentalist parents are likely to be more restrictive when it comes to what TV shows and rap songs their kids can be exposed to. There's also the matter of science: not all fundamentalists read the first chapter of Genesis as a textbook account of the planet's origins, but almost all the people who *do* read Genesis that way are fundamentalists. And there's gender. Fundies are more likely to include "obey" in women's wedding vows (though evangelicals aren't usually radical feminists, either).

One of my professors, who spends most of his scholarly time reading and writing about American Protestantism, has put it this way, only half in jest: a fundamentalist is an evangelical who is angry about something.

Just what is an evangelical, anyway? Different people have answered that question differently. My answer has two parts. First, evangelicals affirm the authority of Scripture. Second, the person of Jesus sits at the center of their faith. Evangelicals understand that they are sinful, that they have been saved from their sin only through Jesus' blood on the Cross. And they prize, in evangelical parlance, *a personal relationship with Jesus.* That is, Jesus is not remote and inaccessible but profoundly involved with the day-to-day lives of his faithful. My Baptist grandmother's favorite hymn makes the point simply:

He walks with me, and He talks with me
And tells me I am his own.

Evangelicals are Christians who are interested in walking and talking with their God, about everything from world peace to car insurance.

But what people *really* want to know when they ask me if I'm an evangelical is whether I vote for Pat Robertson, listen to Amy Grant, and believe the Earth is only five thousand years old. In fact, I've never voted for Pat Roberston, I don't listen to Amy Grant, and I think Darwin might have been on to something.

So, when one of my gin-swilling, scratchy-jazz-listening Columbia comrades asks me the E-question (a question people put to me with alarming frequency), my impulse is to temporize, to hem and haw, to split hairs and explain that my theological orientation is certainly evangelical, but culturally, intellectually, and politically, I am much more sophisticated than the stereotypical evangelical. I'm too insecure about how I'm being perceived to risk correcting my interlocutor's presuppositions—by pointing out, for example, that 33 percent of American evangelicals are registered Democrats, let alone suggesting that not all Republicans or home-schoolers are numbskulls. I simply want to correct his impressions of me: *No, no, I'm not one of them. I'm one of you. I believe that Jesus Christ is Lord, but I also wear fishnet stockings and hang out at the Met.*

I am just as likely as the next person to consign people to tidy categories, and, without much evidence, I assume that my classmate Y. is among what the German theologian Friedrich Schleiermacher called the cultured despisers of religion. I suspect that when Y. asked Z. about my Bible-thumping, he may have been after a little theology—he may have wanted to know if I actually believed the Bible was true—but he was primarily interested in sociology. Y. wanted to know if I was one of *those* people—you know, those tacky, benighted, intolerant types who shun PG–13 movies and own a few polyester pantsuits.

When I look around church on Sunday, I find myself wishing that Y. would ask me himself—*Hey, Lauren, are you one of them? A Bible-thumper? An evangelical?* If he would ask me directly, all my fine parsing would go out the window, and I would simply say, "Yes, of course," even though, on the basis of that answer, Y. would probably assume that I am a Republican who wants to eliminate the National Endowment for the Arts. I would say yes because as I look around All Angels' at a motley crew of evangelicals, some of whom wear polyester and some of whom invite Vera Wang to dinner parties, I know these people are my people.

PHILIP YANCEY

THE "AMPLE" MAN WHO SAVED MY FAITH

(From *Christianity Today*)

If you had asked me during my college years where I would end up, "Christian writer" would fall last on my list of options. I would have recounted the lies my church had told me about race and other matters, and poked fun at its smothering legalism. I would have described an evangelical as a socially stunted wannabe—a fundamentalist with a better income, a slightly more open mind, and a less furrowed brow. I would have complained about the furloughed missionaries who taught classes in science and philosophy at the Bible college I attended and who knew less about those subjects than my high school teachers. That school tended to punish, rather than reward, intellectual curiosity: one teacher admitted he deliberately lowered my grades in order to teach me humility. "The greatest barrier to the Holy Spirit is sophistication," he used to warn his classes.

At that same Bible college, however, I first encountered the writings of C. S. Lewis and G. K. Chesterton. Although separated from me by a vast expanse of sea and culture, they kindled hope that somewhere Christians existed who loosed rather than restrained their minds, who combined sophisticated taste with a humility that did not demean others, and, above all, who experienced life with God as a source of joy and not repression. Ordering tattered used copies through bookshops in England, I devoured everything I could find by these men, one an Oxford don and the other a Fleet Street journalist. As Lewis himself wrote after discovering Chesterton while recovering in a hospital during World War I, "A young man who wishes to remain a strong atheist cannot be too careful of his reading."

Their words sustained me as a lifeline of faith in a sea of turmoil and doubt. I became a writer, I have said, in large part because I realized the power of words in my own life, words that could sail across time and an ocean and quietly, gently, work a transformation of healing and hope. More time would pass before I fully returned to faith, but at least I had models of what life-enhancing faith could look like.

In his story of the Prodigal Son, Jesus does not dwell on the prodigal's motive for return. The younger son feels no sudden remorse or burst of love for the father he insulted. Rather, he tires of a life of squalor and returns out of selfish motives. Apparently, it matters little to God whether we approach him out of desperation or out of longing. *Why did I return?* I ask myself.

My older brother, who played the role of prodigal more

dramatically, demonstrated what could happen if I chose to leave everything behind. In an attempt to break the shackles of a confining upbringing, he went on a grand quest for freedom, trying on worldviews like changes of clothing: Pentecostalism, atheistic existentialism, Buddhism, New Age spirituality, Thomistic rationalism. He joined the flower children of the 1960s, growing his hair long and wearing granny glasses, living communally, experimenting with sex and drugs. For a time he sent me exuberant reports of his new life. Eventually, however, a darker side crept in. I had to bail him out of jail when an LSD trip went bad. He broke relations with every other person in the family and burned through several marriages. I got late-night calls concerning his suicide threats. Watching my brother, I saw up close the destructive power of casting off faith with nothing to take its place.

At the same time, more positively, my career as a journalist gave me the opportunity to investigate people who demonstrate that a connection with God can enlarge, rather than shrink, life. I began the lifelong process of separating church from God. Though I had emerged from childhood churches badly damaged, as I began to scrutinize Jesus through the critical eyes of a journalist, I saw that the qualities that so upset me—legalism, self-righteousness, racism, provincialism, hypocrisy—Jesus had fought against, and were probably the very qualities that led to his crucifixion. Getting to know the God revealed in Jesus, I recognized I needed to change in many ways—yes, even to repent, for I had absorbed the hypocrisy, racism, and self-righteousness of my upbringing and contributed numerous sins of my own. I began to envision God less as a stern judge shaking his finger at my waywardness than as a doctor who prescribes behavior in my best interest in order to safeguard my health.

Surprised by Orthodoxy

"I am the man who with the utmost daring discovered what had been discovered before," G. K. Chesterton declared triumphantly. "I did try to found a heresy of my own, and when I had put the last touches to it, I discovered that it was orthodoxy." Guided in part by Chesterton, I landed in a similar place after a circuitous journey.

When someone asked Chesterton what one book he would want to have along if stranded on a desert island, he paused only an instant before replying, "Why, *A Practical Guide to Shipbuilding*, of course." If I were so stranded, and could choose one book apart from the Bible, I may well select Chesterton's own spiritual autobiography, *Orthodoxy* (1909). Why anyone would pick up a book with that formidable title eludes me, but one day I did so and my faith has never recovered. *Orthodoxy* brought freshness and a new spirit of adventure to my faith as I found odd parallels between my own odyssey and that traveled by its author, a three-hundred-pound, scatterbrained Victorian journalist.

Gilbert Keith Chesterton has sometimes been called "the

master who left no masterpiece," perhaps the curse of his chosen profession. For most of his life (1874–1936) he served as editor of a weekly newspaper of ideas, in the process writing some four thousand essays on topics both trivial and important. He straddled the turn of the century, from the nineteenth to the twentieth, when such movements as modernism, communism, fascism, pacifism, determinism, Darwinism, and eugenics were coming to the fore. As he surveyed each one, he found himself pressed further and further toward Christianity, which he saw as the only redoubt against such potent forces. Eventually he accepted the Christian faith not simply as a bulwark of civilization but rather as an expression of the deepest truths about the world. He took the public step of being baptized into the Roman Catholic church in a mostly Protestant nation.

As a thinker, Chesterton started slowly. By the age of nine, he could barely read, and his parents consulted with a brain specialist about his mental capacity. He dropped out of art school and skipped university entirely. As it turned out, however, he had a memory so prodigious that late in life he could recite the plots of all ten thousand novels he had read and reviewed. He wrote five novels of his own, as well as two hundred short stories, including a series of detective stories centered on Father Brown; tried his hand at plays, poetry, and ballads; wrote literary biographies of such characters as Robert Browning and Charles Dickens; spun off a history of England; and tackled the lives of Francis of Assisi, Thomas Aquinas, and

Jesus himself. Writing at breakneck speed, getting many facts wrong, he nevertheless approached each of his subjects with such discernment, enthusiasm, and wit that even his harshest critics had to stand and applaud.

Chesterton traveled occasionally out of England, and made it across the Atlantic to visit the United States (prompting the book *What I Saw in America*), but mostly he stayed at home, read widely, and wrote about everything that crossed his mind. The rollicking adventures took place inside his great, shaggy head. One can hardly overestimate his impact on others, though. Mahatma Gandhi got many of his ideas on Indian independence from Chesterton; one of his novels inspired Michael Collins's movement for Irish independence; and C. S. Lewis looked to Chesterton as his spiritual father.

Chesterton had been dead more than thirty years when I first discovered him, but he resuscitated my moribund faith. As I look back now, and ask in what way he affected me, I see that he helped awaken in me a sense of long-suppressed joy.

Albert Einstein once articulated the most important question of all: "Is the universe a friendly place?" In childhood and adolescence, I received mixed messages at best. Like the children of alcoholics—who subliminally learn "Don't talk, Don't trust, and Don't feel"—I had responded by flat-lining emotionally. Even as my brother turned outward, launching his grand tour of freedom, I turned inward, sealing off one by one any avenue whereby people could get to me, either to manipulate me or cause pain. I read the novels of Sartre and Camus, whose heroes would stab themselves in the hand or murder someone on the beach just for the experience of it. Especially I read Nietzsche, who described a Superman impervious to suffering. I learned not to laugh or smile, and not to cry.

I see now what I could not see then, that I was erecting a strong stone fortress against love, for I thought myself unlovable. In the most unlikely place, the Bible college I viewed as a kind of asylum, that inner fortress began to crumble. I found solace not in religion, where everyone around me claimed to find it, but in music. Late at night I would steal out of the dormitory and make my way to the chapel and its nine-foot Steinway grand. I never performed in public, but I could passably sight-read Mozart, Chopin, Beethoven, and Schubert, and that is how I spent many evenings, pressing some order into my disordered world. I was creating something, and in spite of myself it seemed beautiful as it echoed through the dark and empty chapel.

Then I fell in love. Janet and I drew together for all the wrong reasons—mainly we sat around and complained about the oppressive atmosphere of the school—but eventually the most powerful force in the universe, love, won out. I had found someone who pointed out everything right with me, not everything wrong. Hope aroused. I wanted to conquer worlds and lay them at her feet. For her birthday I learned Beethoven's *Sonata Pathetique* and asked, trembling, if she would be the very first audience to hear me play. It was an offering to new life, and to her who had called it forth.

The Problem of Pleasure

"The worst moment for the atheist is when he is really thankful and has no one to thank," wrote Chesterton. And also, "Joy, which was the small publicity of the pagan, is the gigantic secret of the Christian." I know well that worst moment and know too the first stirrings of joy that flapped fresh air into crevices long sealed off. Great joy carries within it the intimations of immortality. Suddenly I wanted to live, even to live forever.

Chesterton viewed this world as a sort of cosmic shipwreck. A person in search of meaning resembles a sailor who awakens from a deep sleep and discovers treasure strewn about, relics from a civilization he can barely remember. One by one he picks up the relics—gold coins, a compass, fine clothing—and tries to discern their meaning. Fallen humanity is in such a state. Good things on earth—the natural world, beauty, love, joy—still bear traces of their original purpose, but amnesia mars the image of God in us.

After *Orthodoxy* I read many of Chesterton's other works. (He wrote more than one hundred books, and as a writer it depressed me for weeks to learn that he dictated most of them to his secretary, and made few changes to the first drafts.) I was writing on the problem of pain at the time, and found much insight in *The Man Who Was Thursday* (1907), his fictional treatment of that dark subject. Amazingly, considering their differences in style, he wrote it and *Orthodoxy* during the same year. He later explained that he had been struggling with despair, evil, and the meaning of life, and had even approached mental breakdown. When he emerged from that melancholy, he sought to make a case for optimism amid the gloom of such a world. He had been studying the biblical book of Job, and *Orthodoxy* and *The Man Who Was Thursday* resulted, one a book of apologetics full of unexpected twists and turns, the other best described as a combination spy thriller and nightmare.

In *The Man Who Was Thursday*, Chesterton does not diminish the incaluable mysteries of suffering and free will. Rather, he transforms them into the simplest argument for faith. At its worst, with nature revealing only the backside of God, the universe offers reasons for belief. In God's speech to Job, God pointed to the fierce wildness of nature—the hippopotamus and crocodile, thunderstorms and blizzards, the lioness and mountain goat, untamed oxen and ostriches—and not its friendly side. If nothing else, nature reveals God as mysterious, incalculable, "wholly other," worthy of worship. We may have limited clues to the secrets of reality, but what wondrous clues they are. "Even mere existence, reduced to its most primary limits, was extraordinary enough to be exciting. Anything was magnificent as compared with nothing," Chesterton testified later.

For Chesterton, and also for me, the riddles of God proved more satisfying than the answers proposed without God. I too came to believe in the good things of this world—first revealed to me in music, romantic love, and nature—as relics of a wreck, and as bright clues into the nature of a reality shrouded in darkness. God had answered Job's questions with more questions, as if to say the truths of existence lie far beyond the range of our comprehension. We are left with remnants of God's original design and the freedom, always the freedom, to cast our lots with such a God, or against him.

In addition to the problem of pain, G. K. Chesterton seemed equally fascinated by its opposite, the problem of pleasure. He found materialism too thin to account for the sense of wonder and delight that gives an almost magical dimension to such basic human acts as sex, childbirth, play, and artistic creation.

Why is sex fun? Reproduction surely does not require pleasure: some animals simply split in half to reproduce, and even humans use methods of artificial insemination that involve no pleasure. Why is eating enjoyable? Plants and the lower animals manage to obtain their quota of nutrients without the luxury of taste buds. Why are there colors? Some people get along fine without the ability to detect color. Why complicate vision for all the rest of us?

It struck me, after reading my umpteenth book on the problem of pain, that I have never seen a book on "the problem of pleasure." Nor have I met a philosopher who goes around in head-shaking perplexity over the question of why we experience pleasure. Yet it looms as a huge question—the philosophical equivalent, for atheists, to the problem of pain for Christians. On the issue of pleasure, Christians can breathe easier. A good and loving God would naturally want his creatures to experience delight, joy, and personal fulfillment. Christians start from that assumption and then look for ways to explain the origin of suffering. But should not atheists have an equal obligation to explain the origin of pleasure in a world of randomness and meaninglessness?

Where does pleasure come from? After searching alternatives, Chesterton settled on the Christian answer as the only reasonable explanation for its existence in the world. Moments of pleasure are the remnants washed ashore from a shipwreck, he believed, bits of Paradise extended through time. We must hold these relics lightly, and use them with gratitude and restraint, never seizing them as entitlements.

The churches I attended had stressed the dangers of pleasure so loudly that I missed any positive message. Guided by Chesterton, I came to see sex, money, power, and sensory pleasures as God's good gifts. Every Sunday I can turn on the radio or television and hear preachers decry the drugs, sexual looseness, greed, and crime that are "running rampant" in the streets of America. Rather than merely wag our fingers at such obvious abuses of God's good gifts, perhaps we should demonstrate to the world where good gifts actually come from, and why they are good. Evil's greatest triumph may be its success in portraying religion as an enemy of pleasure when, in fact, religion accounts for pleasure's source: every good and enjoyable thing is the invention of a Creator who lavished gifts on the world.

Prophet of Mirth

"There are an infinity of angles at which one falls, only one at which one stands," said Chesterton, and he ultimately fell from excess, never achieving the balance he preached so convincingly. Not only did he tend to pluck five pears in a mere absence of mind—he ate them. His weight hovered between three hundred and four hundred pounds, and that combined with general poor health to disqualify him from military service, a fact that led to a rather brusque encounter with a patriot during World War I. "Why aren't you out at the front?" demanded the indignant elderly lady when she spied Chesterton on the streets of London. He coolly replied, "My dear madam, if you will step round this way a little, you will see that I am."

That distinctive shape made Chesterton a favorite of London caricaturists. It took only a few strokes for a skilled cartoonist to capture his essence: from the side he looked like a giant capital "P." Chesterton rounded out his reputation with other eccentricities, most of which suited the stereotype of a slovenly, absent-minded professor. He would show up at a wedding wearing no tie and with a price tag on his shoes. Using any available paper, even wallpaper, he would scribble notes when ideas came to him, sometimes standing, oblivious, in the middle of traffic as he did so.

Once he sent his wife this telegram: "Am at Market Harborough. Where ought I to be?"

She telegraphed back, "Home."

Chesterton cheerfully engaged in public debates with agnostics and skeptics of the day, most notably George Bernard Shaw—this at a time when a debate on faith could fill a lecture hall. Chesterton usually arrived late, peered through his *pince-nez* at his disorderly scraps of paper, and proceeded to entertain the crowd, making nervous gestures, fumbling through his pockets, laughing heartily in a falsetto voice at his own jokes.

Typically he would charm the audience over to his side, then celebrate by hosting his chastened opponent at the nearest pub. "Shaw is like the Venus de Milo; all there is of him is admirable," he toasted his friend affectionately.

In Chesterton's day, sober-minded modernists were seeking a new unified theory to explain the past and give hope to the future. Shaw, seeing history as a struggle between the classes, proposed a remedy of socialist utopianism. The early H. G. Wells interpreted history as an evolutionary march toward progress and enlightenment (a view the rest of the century would do much to refute). Sigmund Freud held up a vision of humanity free of repression and the bondage of the unconscious. Ironically, all three of these progressives had in common a rather stern countenance. With furrowed brows and dark, haunted eyes, they would expostulate on their optimistic visions of the future.

Meanwhile, puffing through his incongruously blond moustache, with a pinkly beaming face and a twinkle in his eye, Chesterton would cheerfully defend "reactionary" concepts like original sin and the Last Judgment. Chesterton seemed to sense instinctively that a stern prophet will rarely break through to a society full of religion's "cultured despisers"; he preferred the role of jester.

Chesterton claimed to distrust "hard, cold, thin people," and perhaps that's why I have grown so fond of the jolly fat apologist. Nowadays in the church, sober-mindedness has won the day. Evangelicals can be the kind of responsible citizens most people appreciate as neighbors but don't want to spend much time with. Theologians with long faces lecture on "the imperatives of the faith." The Religious Right calls for moral regeneration, and ordinary Christians point to temperance, industriousness, and achievement as primary proofs of their faith. Could it be that Christians, eager to point out how good we are, neglect the basic fact that the gospel sounds like good news only to bad people?

I have had to forgive the churches I was raised in, much as a person from a dysfunctional family forgives mistakes made by parents and siblings. An irrepressible optimist, G. K. Chesterton proved helpful in that process too. "The Christian ideal has not been tried and found wanting. It has been found difficult and left untried," he said. The real question is not "Why is Christianity so bad when it claims to be so good?" but rather "Why are all human things so bad when they claim to be so good?" Chesterton readily admitted that the church had badly failed the gospel. In fact, he said, one of the strongest arguments in favor of Christianity is the failure of Christians, who thereby prove what the Bible teaches about the Fall and original sin. As the world goes wrong, it proves that the church is right in this basic doctrine.

For this reason, when people tell me their horror stories of growing up in a repressive church environment, I feel no need to defend the actions of the church. The church of my own childhood, as well as that of my present and my future, comprises deeply flawed human beings struggling toward an unattainable ideal. We admit that we will never reach our ideal in this life, a distinctive the church claims that most other human institutions try to deny. Along with Chesterton, I've had to take my place among those who acknowledge that *we* are what is wrong with the world. What is my snobbishness toward my childhood church, for instance, but an inverted form of the harsh judgment it showed me? Whenever faith seems an entitlement, or a measuring rod, we cast our lots with the Pharisees and grace softly slips away.

We could use another Chesterton today, I think. In a time when culture and faith have drifted even further apart, we could use his brilliance, his entertaining style, and above all his generous and joyful spirit.

For all his personal quirkiness, he managed to propound the Christian faith with as much wit, good humor, and sheer intellectual force as anyone in recent times. With the zeal of a knight defending the last redoubt, he took on anyone who dared interpret the world apart from God and Incarnation.

Chesterton himself said that the modern age is characterized by a sadness that calls for a new kind of prophet, not like prophets of old who reminded people that they were going to die, but someone who would remind them they are not dead yet. The prophet of ample girth and ample mirth filled that role splendidly. T. S. Eliot judged, "He did more, I think, than any man of his time . . . to maintain the existence of the important minority in the modern world." I know he did that for me. Whenever I feel my faith going dry again, I wander to a shelf and pick up a book by G. K. Chesterton. The adventure begins all over again.

WENDY MURRAY ZOBA

THE VOICE THAT FOUND HER

(From *Books & Culture*)

She would say that you start with nothing. Then you poke a hole in it and step inside. Then it becomes something. That is where you begin.

In high school she stood in front of a class and refused to speak. It wasn't because she didn't have anything to say. Voices inside her were clamoring to get out. But that classroom was not the place. The teacher threatened to fail her.

She is Diane Glancy, novelist, essayist, playwright, and poet, the daughter of a Cherokee father and a mother whose ancestors were German. She grew up in the white world, but could not assuage the voices of her Native American heritage. At the same time she heard the voice of her stern, goal-oriented German heritage, mainly expressed through her mother. Later there would be the voice of the academician and her Christian voice.

"I can tell several stories at once," she writes in *The Cold-and-Hunger Dance.* "Mixed-blood stories of academic life and the experience of Christianity. Nothing fitting with anything else. The word *community* has always meant being left out." Being a woman didn't help.

She eventually found the one voice that held the others together. Or the voice found her. It came through her writing. The result has been a body of work that defies literary conventions. Critics and marketers prefer writers who are easily categorized. This one is a Novelist, that one a Poet. Glancy not only writes in every familiar genre, she also crosses genres—mixing prose and poetry in the same book, for instance. She's Native American—but unlike many high-profile Native writers, she's also strongly Christian.

If she is hard to categorize, she has nevertheless found readers. Her work has earned her, among other prizes, an American Book Award, a Pushcart Award, and a North American Indian Prose Award. She has received grants from the National Endowment for the Arts and the National Endowment for the Humanities. She has likewise built an academic career; as an associate professor at Macalester College in St. Paul, Minnesota, she teaches creative writing and Native American literature. She is poet laureate of the Five Civilized Tribes. She attends a Bible-believing born-again spirit-filled fundamentalist church.

"The Native believes that the voice is spiritual," she told me when we met in her office last fall. "What you speak actually makes things happen. You tell a story and you empower somebody with knowledge," she says, which might explain in part why she refused to speak that day in her high school classroom. "I had a voice. It carried the pain of my grandmother and father's side, the Cherokee side, the Trail of Tears, the heaviness, the grief, the loss, the disrespect. It was a burden that was there in the voice."

But that was only part of the reason for her self-imposed silence. She also felt the force of her mother's "determined with-it voice," as she calls it. "What are these words I dislike so much? Organization. Goals. Determination. Getting things done. I had two voices and they clashed. I had that storm within me and I was not willing to expose it before everyone. I refused to speak. It was a power I had."

Glancy's father, Lewis Hall, left his Cherokee heritage to assume the life of the white man. He grew up in Arkansas with his mother and sister. During the Depression, he moved to Kansas City to look for work and ended up in the stockyards, where he did well and moved up. Glancy remembers some of the first words he spoke to her: "We're going to live in this world. It's not a bad world." As she writes in *Claiming Breath*, a genre-crossing book of short prose pieces with a flavor of poetry:

He left his heritage to follow this world & I remember the vacuum it made in him. Our heritage doesn't die—It leaves an open gash in need of stitches. Riding in the back seat of our '49 Ford. I watched his black hair—his hands on the wheel. I remember feeling the universe there with us—& at the same time, I remember the hole in our heads where our heritage had once been.

Glancy herself was born dark, like her father. Her mother's people were blond and blue-eyed. "I was a stranger in that group," she says. Her mother, Edith Wood Hall, eschewed the Native heritage of her husband, and her daughter's dark skin strained their relationship. Nor could her mother understand the young girl's mystical inclinations—hearing the voices of her Cherokee ancestors.

At school the young Glancy felt doubly disenfranchised. When she and her classmates studied the Indians they made teepees and feathered war bonnets. But, Indian though she was, she had never seen a war bonnet. And the Cherokee hadn't lived in teepees. They were farmers, not migratory like the Plains Indians. She was Indian in a white culture and a Cherokee in Plains Indian territory. "We were Indian, but not the kind that hunted buffalo."

Her first dynamic encounter with Christianity came as a young girl, when she visited a VBS program sponsored by a local Baptist church. The teacher showed the class a picture of Jesus holding a black sheep. The little Indian girl understood that picture meant that Jesus loved everybody, even the dark ones.

She graduated from high school in 1959 and entered the University of Missouri the following fall. She finished her undergraduate studies five years later, in 1964, the same year she got married in defiance of all the voices.

The next nineteen years were a crucible of struggle. Her husband, an Irishman, succumbed to alcoholism and Glancy was left to raise her two children on her own. Her marriage was like "trying to drive a loaded 18-wheeler up a sandy incline," she writes in *The Cold-and-Hunger Dance*. "There was a voice saying, 'hold on, it will connect and *go somewhere*.'" The voices found release during those hard years. That was when she started writing.

The two novels she wrote during her marriage, *The Only Piece of Furniture in the House* and *Fuller Man*, were both rejected by publishers and filed away. (It would be twenty-five years before they would see the light of day.) Also during that time she completed a collection of short stories and finished her master's degree at Central Oklahoma University in 1983. Her marriage ended that year. "We were in Oklahoma when we divorced and I left him without any money. I had two children. I had nothing."

She had been working for the State Arts Council of Oklahoma, living hand-to-mouth, for several years when she met poet Gerald Stern at a writer's conference. He helped her get an Equal Opportunity Fellowship to attend the University of Iowa's Writer's Workshop, from which she received her MEA in 1988. That year Macalester College called her and asked her to join their faculty. She has been there ever since.

Voices, lost and recovered, give life to the three books closest to Glancy's heart: *Flutie, Pushing the Bear,* and *The Closets of Heaven.*

Thirteen-year-old Flutie Moses, half-white, half-Indian, feels trapped in her provincial, dysfunctional, and seemingly interminable existence in rural Oklahoma. She can't speak to strangers or in public. Her older brother Franklin ends up in jail for stealing car parts (even from his father); her white mother vents her despair over a stifling marriage by putting the pedal to the metal on the back roads of Oklahoma (for which she also does jail time); and her father, a mechanic and a Cherokee, is like a ghost who has lost his story.

The Oklahoma landscape is more than the setting of the book. It assumes a role, like one of the characters. Flutie is driving with her father and brother on a long-coveted road trip to the Salt Plains:

> They passed the glass mountains and red mesas. Here were the voicings, Flutie thought, the tongues of the land, speaking in short bursts of courage before the wind blew the words back into their mouths. Her eyes throbbed. The birds rising on air currents above the bluffs were the words that the land said.

Flutie longs to hear stories from her father about his Native heritage, but he refuses. Her disconsolate mother, on the other hand, is never at a loss for words: "Her mother shot words that hit her." The physical and emotional austerity of Flutie's childhood, along with her mixed heritage and her paralyzing shyness, causes her to retreat into a world of visions and fantasies:

> Sometimes in the darkness inside her head, she could see an opening above her. She could see figures looking down at her from the opening. They were Elders. Helpers. She knew it. Maybe they were the Indian people of her father's tribe who were gone, but they were still there.

At fifteen, Flutie still has not overcome her demons. "Open my mouth that I might speak. That was what she wanted each year in school. Release." At seventeen she turns to drugs and alcohol to find it. "She had a voice somewhere inside her. She could feel it moving."

When she refuses to marry her high-school boyfriend, her mother kicks her out of the house. She takes a loan to attend college and leaves for the city: "Flutie drove the truck and cried as she drove. . . . She had to speak a road into being, but the words would not come. Maybe someday they would."

Flutie finally finds her voice one day in a college classroom:

> It was Flutie's turn to work through an algebra problem on the board. In speaking, Flutie felt the storm hit. The water pounded her head. She felt her unsteady knees. . . .
>
> The Great Spirit reached down and poked her throat open and let out the lava. She was in the power of her voice.

She spoke the boiling words. Her whole being rocked. Her
head spasmed. She sat down. The room shook with her. But
it was done. . . . She traveled in her head all that day. She
would speak in the next class and the next. Tongues would
fill her mouth. Soon she wouldn't be able to wait for her turn.

. . .

Where Flutie gives voice to an individual consciousness,
unforgettably distinct, *Pushing the Bear* gives voice to an entire
community, the Cherokee who walked the Trail of Tears in
1838–39. Glancy describes this communal storytelling in *The
Cold-and-Hunger Dance:*

Native American storying is an act of gathering many
voices to tell a story in many different ways. One voice
alone is not enough because we are what we are in relationship to others, and we each have our different way of
seeing. Native American writing is also an alignment of
voices so the story comes through.

Pushing the Bear "stories" the Trail of Tears through a multi-
tude of narrators, some historical, others fictional.

The book opens with an epigraph that reads: "From October 1838 through February 1839 some eleven to thirteen
thousand Cherokee walked nine hundred miles in bitter cold
from the southeast to Indian Territory. One fourth died or
disappeared along the way." The parents of Glancy's great-

grandfather, Woods Lewis (born in 1843), were numbered among those who walked the Trail.

Her inspiration came in the late 1970s when she saw a dramatization of the Trail in Tahlequah, Oklahoma. In the mid–1980s she traveled to New Echota, Georgia, where the Treaty of New Echota was signed by a few Cherokee relinquishing the eastern lands of them all. "When you write as a Native writer you've got to be on the land because the land is the first thing that speaks," she says. Glancy was on the grounds of New Echota when she heard the voice of the novel's main character, Maritole: "I knew she was sitting on her cabin steps. I knew she looked over the dried corn stalks and I knew there was a cloud of dust and the soldiers were coming."

It took Glancy nearly twenty years to complete this book, partly because her Cherokee kinsmen did not want her to write it. "They said, 'Don't write that book. Speaking brings it back into being. We don't want to hear that.'" Beyond that, the historical record was skimpy. "Not a lot was written about it or left behind because the Indians were ashamed of it and the government was ashamed."

There were stretches when she would put her research away and work on other projects. In time, however, "those voices would begin to rumble around. They wanted to be told and I knew they did." So she pressed on. Her research included traveling the same nine-hundred-mile trek that her ancestors had walked.

An important subtext of the book is Glancy's examination of the role of Christianity in the lives of the Cherokee and—in view of their tortured circumstances on the Trail—their treatment at the hands of the Christian white man. The many narrators represent varying degrees of belief or unbelief, both in the Christian God and the traditional gods of the Cherokee.

Maritole's father has lost hope in the power of the tribal magic: "I had made a trap to protect our cabin. I removed the brain of a yellow mockingbird . . . put it into a hollowed gourd, buried it in front of the door. But the soldiers came anyway. Now we are walking."

The Reverend Jesse Bushyhead, a Native half-breed and an historical figure, preached a sermon about halfway along the Trail:

> "I hear the spirits with us. We are not abandoned. At night I hear the angels groaning under the weight of their wings. We can't see them—no—" I shook my head. "They're rolling our wagons on the long path to the new territory. We're wheezing and jerking and spilling our way. . . . Does not our blood stain the snow?" My voice cracked. Not since the smallpox epidemics had so many died. Even the animals dragging the wagons collapsed. . . .
>
> "We look at our sorrow and know it's not all," I reminded. "Somewhere people are warm and singing in their churches. We will again. Our children. Some will survive. We are the land. We'll have a remnant—We'll—" I coughed back my

grief and began at another place. "Our journey—the one ahead—the one after this walking—will begin again from nothing. This is how we go. Always back to nothing." I stumbled as if my words were a bundle I carried. As if I were top-heavy with my sermon.

And Maritole's broken and despairing husband, Knobowtee, reflects near the trail's end:

There was a voice somewhere. With all the voices on the trail. Ancestors. Conjurers. People. Even the voices of the animals and the land. I was almost sure I heard a voice. You brought us through the fire and through the water— Maybe it was Bushyhead preaching in his sleep. . . . Maybe it was a voice beyond hope. A certainty I could hear in the ministers' voices. It woke me in the night. There was something that made sense. I just couldn't see it. But look at the churches in the towns we passed. It was their God. Those people who made the Cherokee walk.

The tug of war in this book over matters of faith reflects Glancy's own struggle in trying to reconcile her Native heritage with her Christian beliefs. "It is a hard lump to swallow, the enemy bringing this message," she says. "I hear [the Cherokee] say all the time, 'They stole our land. They stole our culture,' and it's true." Still, she says, "The white culture brought Christ, and that is one thing the Native Americans would never have known. Many Natives don't want to hear it. They want to follow their own way and do things in their own strength." She writes in *Claiming Breath:*

> I think the sacred hoop of the Indian nation was broken because it wasn't the sacred hoop of God. It wasn't complete. It left too much to pride & self works. . . . & the incompleteness of the sacred hoop before God was made evident & it was broken by the white man with his terrible ways. His repeating rifles & broken treaties & all the treachery that is in the human heart.
>
> Yet in that imperfect vehicle came news of the light. That is a hard lesson.

She has reconciled these voices through her writing. For example, in *The West Pole,* she likens the Christian faith to the Native understanding of the horse:

> When the Native American saw the horse he called it Sacred Dog. Or the Medicine Dog. It came to define wholeness for the Native American. When two-rode-as-one. Or when the horse's shadow and your shadow were one. That's what it feels like to receive the light of Christ and ride on in faith.

She returned to the Cherokee people once *Pushing the Bear* was complete to do a reading. It was the hardest reading she has given, she says. "They don't give you much recognition by voice. But they sat there nodding. It was accepted very well."

To give voice to her ancestors who walked the Trail, Glancy had to listen across the span of two centuries. In *The Closets of Heaven,* she is even more audacious. Here she goes back two thousand years to recover the voice of the biblical character Dorcas (Acts 9:36–43), the voice of one called back from death to life.

Dorcas confesses early in the book, "Sewing is my prayer." She is confused by talk among her fellow Christians about being saved by faith alone:

> By faith I am saved. By faith. That's what they say Peter preaches. But salvation is also by works. That's what I want. When I sew, the power of God is undeniable. I feel my thoughts as I sit in the dark. I have purpose. I have something to do.

As she ponders these things, she feels a dull pain that eventually becomes acute to the point of death. Then Dorcas enters heaven:

> I see there are closets in heaven. Full of shawls and mantles. . . . I see the transformation of cloth. The resurrection of sewing. . . . Beyond the closets, I see a vast city of people. Streets. A river. Somewhere a throne. I see

heaven full of flying beings. Birds. Crowned pigeons. Their eyes red as heaven. . . . Closets of garments I have sewn. I cannot explain. I wish I had used more than one thread on a needle. Threads of different colors. Why didn't I know? . . . I want to rework all I have sewed. I see the garments differently now, I see them as garments within garments.

She hears her name—not in its Greek form, Dorcas, but rather in Aramaic, her mother-tongue: *Tabitha.* "I open my eyes and see the disciple. I know he is Peter. The power of his word pulls me. I am on the shores of heaven when I hear his voice. . . . Peter has my hand: I draw it back. I want to snip off his arm, but I remember I must be polite."

She spends the rest of her resurrected days enduring the questions of fellow widows. What was it like to die? What is heaven like? Why can't you describe it better?

I want to cry, but I will not let the tears run down my face. We don't always get to do what we want, I tell myself. But I am angry. The first time I was going someplace, I was returned to Joppa. . . . How dare Peter bring me back? How dare the other widows ask him to call me? I was in heaven. . . . Why couldn't they leave me alone? . . . What do I do now? Tolerate these women? Wait for another death? . . . Whose idea was it?

Like most of the principal characters in Glancy's fiction, Dorcas is an ordinary woman. "I speak ordinary things into being, like the common woman with an ordinary life," Glancy says. "I wasn't a king. I had not gone to war. I was a woman without much of a voice. I was nothing. But I would make something of the nothing."

Language is Glancy's tool for building something out of that nothing. She stretches it, she says in *The Cold-and-Hunger Dance*, to accommodate the voices of minorities and women. The Native voice expresses itself in rhythms and cadence. Her use of imagery borders on mystical. One reviewer said *Flutie* reads almost like a myth. A reader told me that her books ought to be sung.

Women's voices, Glancy says, are often not "strong and forward moving," so she accommodates that with a meandering style. She makes no apologies for inordinate use of the passive voice. "It is circular, indirect, fluid, dreamlike, and intuitive. It speaks from the heart. It is the holding together of language in your own original expression," she says.

But the story is a force beyond the words themselves that exists in its own right. She hears it, gives it form through language, and it thus imbues the reader or hearer with its power: "It is the spirit of storytelling, rather than the artifact of the story itself, that goes forth. It's an energy field that generates power and does not die." She likens it to God, who, independent of the physical expressions of his world, can say, "I am that I am."

Having found her voice, Glancy doesn't take it for granted. She is working on three new novels. One is a "white novel" about an older woman whose husband has Alzheimer's. Another is a Native novel, with the working title *Designs of the Night Sky*, in which she uses a creation story to animate the origins of written language: "The Native believes the voice is spiritual and the written word has killed the voice, nailing it on the page. This book is a story of the written word moving around in the night sky like the constellations, and how it is important too." Finally, she is at work on another fictional biblical narrative, inspired by the account of the four daughters of Philip who prophesied (Acts 21:9). "Their names are not given. What were those four women like?"

To claim breath, to find one's own voice, Glancy teaches us, requires attentiveness to the voices of others. She's listening.

LIONEL BASNEY was professor of English at Calvin College at the time of his accidental death in 1999. His essay "Immanuel's Ground," also from *The American Scholar*, appeared in *Best Christian Writing* 2000.

JOSEPH BOTTUM is books and arts editor of *The Weekly Standard*, host of *Book Talk*, a nationally syndicated radio program, and the author of *The Fall & Other Poems*. His essay "Pius XII and the Nazis" appeared in *Best Christian Writing* 2001.

PAUL ELIE is an editor at Farrar, Straus and Giroux and the editor of a collection of essays, *A Tremor of Bliss: Contemporary Writers on the Sacraments*. His book *The Life You Save May be Your Own*, on Thomas Merton, Dorothy Day, Walker Percy, and Flannery O'Connor, is forthcoming.

SARAH E. HINLICKY is a student at Princeton Theological Seminary. Her essay "Seminary Sanity" appeared in *Best Christian Writing* 2001.

DONALD JUEL is Richard J. Dearborn professor of New Testament at Princeton Theological Seminary. His many books include several on the Gospel of Mark.

GARRET KEIZER is the author of three books of nonfiction, *No Place But Here*, *A Dresser of Sycamore Trees*, and most recently *The Enigma of Anger: Essays on a Sometimes Deadly Sin*, as well as a novel, *God Of Beer*. He lives in northeastern Vermont with his wife and daughter.

RICHARD LISCHER served fourteen years as a Lutheran pastor and now teaches at Duke University Divinity School. Among his books are *The Preacher King: Martin Luther King, Jr. and the Word That Moved America* and a memoir, *Open Secrets: A Spiritual Journey Through a Country Church*, from which his essay in this volume is adapted.

WILFRED M. MCCLAY holds the SunTrust Chair of Excellence in Humanities at the University of Tennessee at Chattanooga, and is the author most recently of *The Student's Guide to U.S. History*. His essays and reviews appear frequently in *The Wilson Quarterly*, *First Things*, and other publications.

FREDERICA MATHEWES-GREEN is a columnist and commentator whose work has appeared in magazines such as *Christianity Today* and *Our Sunday Visitor* (where she reviews movies), online at beliefnet.com and other sites, and on the air via National Public Radio. She is also the author of several books that have introduced the Orthodox faith to American readers, including most recently *The Illumined Heart: The Ancient Christian Path of Transformation*. Her essay "A Cold Day in December" appeared in *Best Christian Writing* 2000.

GILBERT MEILAENDER holds the Phyllis and Richard Duesenberg Chair in Christian Ethics at Valparaiso University. He is the author of a number of books, including *Things That Count: Essays Moral and Theological*. His essay on vocation, "Divine Summons," also from *The Christian Century*, appeared in *Best Christian Writing* 2001.

JÜRGEN MOLTMANN is professor of theology at the University of Tübingen and one of the most influential theologians of the past half-century. Among the latest of his books to appear in English is *The Spirit of Life: A Universal Affirmation*.

RICHARD JOHN NEUHAUS is editor-in-chief of *First Things* and head of the Institute for Religion and Public Life. His most recent books include *As I Lay Dying: A Meditation Upon Returning* and *The Chosen People in an Almost Chosen Nation: Jews and Judaism in America* (a collection he edited). He has had essays in both previous volumes of *Best Christian Writing* as well as in this year's volume.

EUGENE PETERSON was for many years pastor of Christ Our King United Presbyterian Church in Bel Air, Maryland; he has also served as professor of spiritual theology at Regent

College in Vancouver, B.C. He is the author of many books, including *A Long Obedience in the Same Direction: Discipleship in an Instant Society* and *Leap Over the Wall: Earthy Spirituality for Everyday Christians*, based on the life of David. This year, his rendering of the Bible, *The Message*, appeared for the first time complete in one volume.

CORNELIUS PLANTINGA, JR., is President of Calvin Theological Seminary and the author most recently of *Engaging God's Word: A Christian Vision of Faith, Learning, and Living*.

GABRIEL SAID REYNOLDS is a doctoral student in Islamic studies at Yale University.

DEBRA RIENSTRA is professor of English at Calvin College and the author of *Great with Child: Reflections on Faith, Fullness, and Becoming a Mother*, from which her essay in this volume is taken.

AMY SCHWARTZ is a journalist and a member of the editorial board of *The Washington Post*. Her essay in this volume was the winning entry in a contest co-sponsored by HarperCollins and beliefnet.com, in which contestants were asked to update C.S. Lewis's classic work, *The Screwtape Letters*, with a letter of their own in the spirit of Lewis's original.

NANCY HASTINGS SEHESTED is a Baptist preacher and state prison chaplain in the mountains of North Carolina.

BARBARA BROWN TAYLOR is an Episcopal priest (many of whose sermons have been collected and published) and former rector of Grace-Calvary Episcopal Church in Clarkesville, Georgia. Currently she holds the Harry R. Butman Chair in Religion and Philosophy at Piedmont College. Her most recent book is *Speaking of Sin: The Lost Language of Salvation*.

SAM TORODE is art and design director of *Touchstone* magazine and an independent illustrator and designer. With his wife, Bethany, he is the author of *Open Embrace: A Protestant Couple Rethinks Contraception*.

WALTER WANGERIN, JR., is Emil and Elfrieda Jochum Professor of Creative Writing and Theology at Valparaiso University. He is the author of dozens of books across many genres. Among his most recent are *Paul: A Novel* and *Swallowing the Golden Stone: Stories and Essays*.

LAUREN F. WINNER is a doctoral student in the history of American religion at Columbia University. She is the author of the memoir *Girl Meets God: On the Path to a Religious Life* and, with Randall Balmer, *Protestantism in America*. Her essay "Good Shabbess" appeared in *Best Christian Writing* 2000.

PHILIP YANCEY is the author of many books, including most recently *Soul Survivor: How My Faith Survived the Church*, from

which his essay in this volume is adapted. He wrote the introduction for *Best Christian Writing* 2000, the first volume in the
series, and his essay "Living with Furious Opposites," also from
Christianity Today, appeared in last year's volume.

WENDY MURRAY ZOBA is the author of *Day of Reckoning:
Columbine and the Search for America's Soul* and *Sacred Journeys*. Her
articles appear in *The Christian Century*, *Christianity Today*, and
other publications.

READER'S DIRECTORY

For more information about or subscriptions to the periodicals represented in The Best Christian Writing 2002, please contact:

The American Scholar
The Phi Beta Kappa Society
1785 Massachusetts Avenue, NW, Fourth Floor
Washington, DC 20036

beliefnet.com
www.beliefnet.com

Books & Culture
465 Gundersen Drive
Carol Stream, IL 60188

boundless.com
www.boundless.com

Christian Century
104 S. Michigan Avenue
Chicago, IL 60603–5901

Christianity Today
465 Gundersen Drive
Carol Stream, IL 60188

First Things
The Insitute on Religion and Public Life
156 Fifth Avenue, Suite 400
New York, NY 10010

Harper's
666 Broadway
New York, NY 10012

Leadership
465 Gundersen Drive
Carol Stream, IL 60188

Perspectives
Office of Research Development and Administration
Southern Illinois University
Carbondale, IL 62901

Soujourners
2401 15th Street, NW
Washington, DC 20009

Theology Today
P.O. Box 821
Princeton, NJ 08542

Touchstone
The Fellowship of St. James
P.O. Box 410788
Chicago, IL 60641

The Weekly Standard
1150 17th Street, NW
Suite 505
Washington, DC 20036